DISCARD

DATE DUE

1/3			

DEMCO 128-5046

CYRUS THE GREAT

◆ ◆ ◆

❖ ANCIENT WORLD LEADERS ❖

CYRUS
THE GREAT

SAMUEL WILLARD CROMPTON

CHELSEA HOUSE
PUBLISHERS
An imprint of Infobase Publishing

Frontis: Engraving of Cyrus the Great.

Chelsea House
An imprint of Infobase Publishing
132 West 31st Street
New York, NY 10001

Library of Congress Cataloging-in-Publication Data

Crompton, Samuel Willard.
  Cyrus the Great / Samuel Willard Crompton.
    p. cm. — (Ancient world leaders)
  Includes bibliographical references and index.
  ISBN-13: 978-0-7910-9636-9 (hardcover)
  1. Cyrus, King of Persia, d. 529 B.C. 2. Achaemenid dynasty, 559–330 B.C. 3. Iran—kings and rulers—Biography. I. Title.
  DS282.C76 2006
  935'.05092—dc22   2007050076

Chelsea House books are available at special discounts when purchased in bulk quantities for businesses, associations, institutions, or sales promotions. Please call our Special Sales Department in New York at (212) 967-8800 or (800) 322-8755.

You can find Chelsea House on the World Wide Web at http://www.chelseahouse.com

Text design by Lina Farinella
Cover design by Jooyoung An

Printed in the United States of America

Bang NMSG 10 9 8 7 6 5 4 3 2 1

This book is printed on acid-free paper.

All links and Web addresses were checked and verified to be correct at the time of publication. Because of the dynamic nature of the Web, some addresses and links may have changed since publication and may no longer be valid.

❖ CONTENTS ❖

Arthur M. Schlesinger, Jr.
On Leadership

Leadership, it may be said, is really what makes the world go round. Love no doubt smoothes the passage; but love is a private transaction between consenting adults. Leadership is a public transaction with history. The idea of leadership affirms the capacity of individuals to move, inspire, and mobilize masses of people so that they act together in pursuit of an end. Sometimes leadership serves good purposes, sometimes bad; but whether the end is benign or evil, great leaders are those men and women who leave their personal stamp on history.

Now, the very concept of leadership implies the proposition that individuals can make a difference. This proposition has never been universally accepted. From classical times to the present day, eminent thinkers have regarded individuals as no more than the agents and pawns of larger forces, whether the gods and goddesses of the ancient world or, in the modern era, race, class, nation, the dialectic, the will of the people, the spirit of the times, history itself. Against such forces, the individual dwindles into insignificance.

So contends the thesis of historical determinism. Tolstoy's great novel *War and Peace* offers a famous statement of the case. Why, Tolstoy asked, did millions of men in the Napoleonic Wars, denying their human feelings and their common sense, move back and forth across Europe slaughtering their fellows? "The war," Tolstoy answered, "was bound to happen simply because it was bound to happen." All prior history determined it. As for leaders, they, Tolstoy said, "are but the labels that serve to give a name to an end and, like labels, they have the least possible connection with the event." The greater the leader, "the more conspicuous the inevitability and the predestination of every act he commits." The leader, said Tolstoy, is "the slave of history."

Determinism takes many forms. Marxism is the determinism of class. Nazism the determinism of race. But the idea of men and women as the slaves of history runs athwart the deepest human instincts. Rigid determinism abolishes the idea of human freedom—the assumption of free choice that underlies every move we make, every word we speak, every thought we think. It abolishes the idea of human responsibility, since it is manifestly unfair to reward or punish people for actions that are by definition beyond their control. No one can live consistently by any deterministic creed. The Marxist states prove this themselves by their extreme susceptibility to the cult of leadership.

More than that, history refutes the idea that individuals make no difference. In December 1931 a British politician crossing Fifth Avenue in New York City between 76th and 77th Streets around 10:30 p.m. looked in the wrong direction and was knocked down by an automobile— a moment, he later recalled, of a man aghast, a world aglare: "I do not understand why I was not broken like an eggshell or squashed like a gooseberry." Fourteen months later an American politician, sitting in an open car in Miami, Florida, was fired on by an assassin; the man beside him was hit. Those who believe that individuals make no difference to history might well ponder whether the next two decades would have been the same had Mario Constasino's car killed Winston Churchill in 1931 and Giuseppe Zangara's bullet killed Franklin Roosevelt in 1933. Suppose, in addition, that Lenin had died of typhus in Siberia in 1895 and that Hitler had been killed on the western front in 1916. What would the 20th century have looked like now?

For better or for worse, individuals do make a difference. "The notion that a people can run itself and its affairs anonymously," wrote the philosopher William James, "is now well known to be the silliest of absurdities. Mankind does nothing save through initiatives on the part of inventors, great or small, and imitation by the rest of us—these are the sole factors in human progress. Individuals of genius show the way, and set the patterns, which common people then adopt and follow."

Leadership, James suggests, means leadership in thought as well as in action. In the long run, leaders in thought may well make the greater difference to the world. "The ideas of economists and political philosophers, both when they are right and when they are wrong," wrote John Maynard Keynes, "are more powerful than is commonly understood. Indeed the world is ruled by little else. Practical men, who believe themselves to be quite exempt from any intellectual influences, are usually the slaves of some defunct economist. . . . The power of vested interests is vastly exaggerated compared with the gradual encroachment of ideas."

But, as Woodrow Wilson once said, "Those only are leaders of men, in the general eye, who lead in action. . . . It is at their hands that new thought gets its translation into the crude language of deeds." Leaders in thought often invent in solitude and obscurity, leaving to later generations the tasks of imitation. Leaders in action—the leaders portrayed in this series—have to be effective in their own time.

And they cannot be effective by themselves. They must act in response to the rhythms of their age. Their genius must be adapted, in a phrase from William James, "to the receptivities of the moment." Leaders are useless without followers. "There goes the mob," said the French politician, hearing a clamor in the streets. "I am their leader. I must follow them." Great leaders turn the inchoate emotions of the mob to purposes of their own. They seize on the opportunities of their time, the hopes, fears, frustrations, crises, potentialities. They succeed when events have prepared the way for them, when the community is awaiting to be aroused, when they can provide the clarifying and organizing ideas. Leadership completes the circuit between the individual and the mass and thereby alters history.

It may alter history for better or for worse. Leaders have been responsible for the most extravagant follies and most monstrous crimes that have beset suffering humanity. They have also been vital in such gains as humanity has made in individual freedom, religious and racial tolerance, social justice, and respect for human rights.

There is no sure way to tell in advance who is going to lead for good and who for evil. But a glance at the gallery of men and women in ANCIENT WORLD LEADERS suggests some useful tests.

One test is this: Do leaders lead by force or by persuasion? By command or by consent? Through most of history leadership was exercised by the divine right of authority. The duty of followers was to defer and to obey. "Theirs not to reason why/ Theirs but to do and die." On occasion, as with the so-called enlightened despots of the 18th century in Europe, absolutist leadership was animated by humane purposes. More often, absolutism nourished the passion for domination, land, gold, and conquest and resulted in tyranny.

The great revolution of modern times has been the revolution of equality. "Perhaps no form of government," wrote the British historian James Bryce in his study of the United States, *The American Commonwealth*, "needs great leaders so much as democracy." The idea that all people should be equal in their legal condition has undermined the old structure of authority, hierarchy, and deference. The revolution of equality has had two contrary effects on the nature of leadership. For equality, as Alexis de Tocqueville pointed out in his great study *Democracy in America*, might mean equality in servitude as well as equality in freedom.

"I know of only two methods of establishing equality in the political world," Tocqueville wrote. "Rights must be given to every citizen, or none at all to anyone . . . save one, who is the master of all." There was no middle ground "between the sovereignty of all and the absolute power of one man." In his astonishing prediction of 20th-century totalitarian dictatorship, Tocqueville explained how the revolution of equality could lead to the *Führerprinzip* and more terrible absolutism than the world had ever known.

But when rights are given to every citizen and the sovereignty of all is established, the problem of leadership takes a new form, becomes more exacting than ever before. It is easy to issue commands and enforce them by the rope and the stake, the concentration camp and the *gulag*. It is much harder to use argument and achievement to overcome opposition and win consent. The Founding Fathers of the United States understood the difficulty. They believed that history had given them the opportunity to decide, as Alexander Hamilton wrote in the first Federalist Paper, whether men are indeed capable of basing government on "reflection and choice, or whether they are forever destined to depend . . . on accident and force."

Government by reflection and choice called for a new style of leadership and a new quality of followership. It required leaders to be responsive to popular concerns, and it required followers to be active and informed participants in the process. Democracy does not eliminate emotion from politics; sometimes it fosters demagoguery; but it is confident that, as the greatest of democratic leaders put it, you cannot fool all of the people all of the time. It measures leadership by results and retires those who overreach or falter or fail.

It is true that in the long run despots are measured by results too. But they can postpone the day of judgment, sometimes indefinitely, and in the meantime they can do infinite harm. It is also true that democracy is no guarantee of virtue and intelligence in government, for the voice of the people is not necessarily the voice of God. But democracy, by assuring the right of opposition, offers built-in resistance to the evils inherent in absolutism. As the theologian Reinhold Niebuhr summed it up, "Man's capacity for justice makes democracy possible, but man's inclination to justice makes democracy necessary."

A second test for leadership is the end for which power is sought. When leaders have as their goal the supremacy of a master race or the promotion of totalitarian revolution or the acquisition and exploitation of colonies or the protection of greed and privilege or the preservation of personal power, it is likely that their leadership will do little to advance the cause of humanity. When their goal is the abolition of slavery, the liberation of women, the enlargement of opportunity for the poor and powerless, the extension of equal rights to racial minorities, the defense of the freedoms of expression and opposition, it is likely that their leadership will increase the sum of human liberty and welfare.

Leaders have done great harm to the world. They have also conferred great benefits. You will find both sorts in this series. Even "good" leaders must be regarded with a certain wariness. Leaders are not demigods; they put on their trousers one leg after another just like ordinary mortals. No leader is infallible, and every leader needs to be reminded of this at regular intervals. Irreverence irritates leaders but is their salvation. Unquestioning submission corrupts leaders and demeans followers. Making a cult of a leader is always a mistake. Fortunately, hero worship generates its own antidote. "Every hero," said Emerson, "becomes a bore at last."

The single benefit the great leaders confer is to embolden the rest of us to live according to our own best selves, to be active, insistent, and resolute in affirming our own sense of things. For great leaders attest to the reality of human freedom against the supposed inevitabilities of history. And they attest to the wisdom and power that may lie within the most unlikely of us, which is why Abraham Lincoln remains the supreme example of great leadership. A great leader, said Emerson, exhibits new possibilities to all humanity. "We feed on genius. . . . Great men exist that there may be greater men."

Great leaders, in short, justify themselves by emancipating and empowering their followers. So humanity struggles to master its destiny, remembering with Alexis de Tocqueville: "It is true that around every man a fatal circle is traced beyond which he cannot pass; but within the wide verge of that circle he is powerful and free; as it is with man, so with communities." ◆

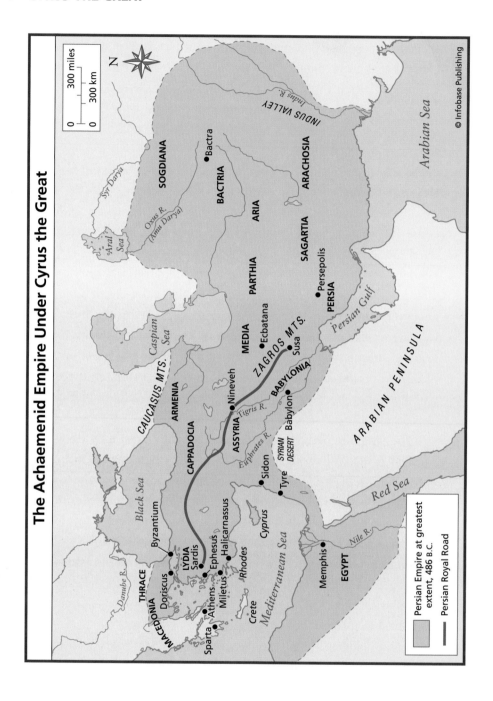

The Achaemenid Empire Under Cyrus the Great

1

An American in Persia

IN 1903, A.V. WILLIAMS JACKSON, A PROFESSOR OF PERSIAN LANGUAGES AT Columbia University, received a sabbatical that allowed him to go to the land of kings, queens, prophets, and shepherds. Persia, its peoples and languages, formed the basis for Professor Jackson's lifelong studies: He now delighted in being able to see so many sites firsthand.

Arriving in northern Persia (the country name was changed to Iran in 1935) in March, Professor Jackson made his way by horse and cart through the northern lands that had once belonged to Cyrus the Great. The professor was deeply interested in Cyrus and other leading Persian kings, but he was also fascinated by the life and teachings of the prophet Zoroaster.

Professor Jackson longed to meet modern-day Zoroastrians, though he knew they were few in number.

Coming south from the Caucasus Mountains, Professor Jackson came to the modern city of Hamadan. He was disappointed that so little of its ancient grandeur had been preserved; indeed, it has been the lament of archaeologists ever since. But, just 20 miles outside Hamadan was the rock carving at Behistun, rightly considered one of the marvels of the ancient world.

High on a cliff that overlooks the main road—the same one Cyrus and his successors created—the rock of Behistun is about 700 feet above the plain and about 2,500 feet above sea level (much of Iran is at 4,000 feet above sea level, and there are mountains as high as 20,000 feet). Here, two-thirds of the way up the massive cliff, Darius I, King of Kings, had his stone carvers give him immortality. Their task was to depict Darius and nine defeated rebels, each of whom had come to a bad end.

The carver, or carvers, did a magnificent job. The rock carving, according to Professor Jackson, was "as perfect as when the stone-cutter of Darius laid his mallet aside. No granite tablet in Central Park or Trafalgar Square could be more perfect." A careful observer, Professor Jackson measured the carving itself, then the cuneiform letters, or symbols, carved below. The inscription was written in three different languages: Old Persian, Elamite, and Babylonian. This did not surprise him, for he knew Darius I, King of Kings, presided over an immense, multinational empire, where many languages were spoken. But the beauty of the carving, and the way it had been preserved—rather than destroyed—by nature, took Professor Jackson's breath away.

Intrigued as he was by the carving, Professor Jackson was also interested in the script, for it spoke of the great god Ahuramazda, leader of the Zoroastrian pantheon. Other scholars had translated these words before, but few had had such

This rock relief of Darius, carved 325 feet (100 meters) above the ground, illustrates his conquering of his enemies to fulfill his destiny as ruler of Persia. Inscribed with the story of how Darius was divinely chosen to rule the Persian Empire, this carving can be found on a road that connects the capitals of Babylon and Media, two other ancient civilizations.

a combined interest in both the Persian king and the Persian prophet:

> Thus saith Darius the King: Those countries which became rebellious, the Lie made them rebellious, so that they deceived the people. Ahuramazda delivered them into my hand. . . . Thus saith Darius the King: That which I have done

I have done altogether by the grace of Ahuramazda. Thou
who shalt hereafter read this inscription, let that which hath
been done by me appear to thee true; hold it not for a lie.

To lie was the worst thing a Persian could do. False words
corrupted the spirit of that individual and lessened the strength
of good in the universe. According to the prophet Zoroaster,
the entire universe was in a perpetual battle between good and
evil, and men and women must speak the truth, as part of their
contribution toward helping the powers of light defeat those of
darkness.

Leaving Behistun, Professor Jackson rode to the south, but
for at least 20 miles of travel he could turn back and still see the
massive cliff recede. This visit was among the most memorable
of his six months in Persia.

THE TOMB OF CYRUS

About two weeks after leaving Behistun, Professor Jackson
came to the area famed as the burial place of Cyrus the Great.
Long had Professor Jackson waited for this moment; he had
spoken to enough other travelers to believe this would be one
of the highlights of his trip.

Parsagadae, or the home of the Persians, is situated in the
southern part of the Zagros Mountains, which separate Iran
from Iraq. Those mountains also keep out what would other-
wise be the encroachment of the desert plains of eastern Iraq.
Like many who had come before, Professor Jackson had to ride
up into the mountains to come to Parsagadae:

An hour's easy ride, crossing once or twice the intersecting
channels of the Polvar [River], or ancient Medus, brought
me to the foot of the ridge. The ascent was rough, but not at
all difficult, and as the horses surmounted the rocky crest a
sharp bend in the old caravan road threw open to view the

historic Plain of Murghab in all its rich fertility, spreading its green expanse fully nine miles in one direction and fifteen in another.

Green is a word not often associated with Iran, which is high, hot, and dry. But the ancient Persians and the modern-day Iranians did their best to change this "condition" through adroit use of irrigation systems. Persians love their gardens, and the very word *paradise* came to the English language from Persian, with Greek serving as an intermediate step.

Several hundred yards farther southward is a solitary shaft, nearly twenty feet high and broken at the top. It is composed of three blocks, as shown by my photograph, and looks as if it might have formed part of a doorway. Near the summit of this column are carved in cuneiform script, in three languages, the simple but dignified words, 'I am Cyrus the King, the Achamenian'—**ADAM KURUSH KHSHAYATIHIYA HAKHAMANISHIYA.**

Professor Jackson felt considerable excitement. He had come so far, and was finally seeing the closest that modern-day humans have to a record of Cyrus the Great. But he pushed on a little farther to see a monolith:

This impressive monument is a huge slab, over twelve feet high, five feet broad, and about two feet in thickness. Upon its weathered front is carved in low relief the figure of a king. On his head there rests a curious crown which shows traces of the influence of Egyptian art; but the most striking features of the image is a double set of immense fanlike wings that rise from the shoulders and droop almost to the feet. The sculptured form is the very idealization of sovereignty. The top of the monolith, which once was inscribed, is broken off, but the missing device, as we know from the drawings of the earlier travelers, consisted of the simple words, 'I am Cyrus the King, the Achaemenian'—in keeping with the dignity of the surroundings.

Professor Jackson was neither the first nor the last traveler to remark on the beauty of this monument, which shows a winged man (or genie) facing the viewer's right. Many historians and archaeologists have mused over this particular sculpture, thinking it might be a portrait of the actual Cyrus, but the consensus of most archaeologists is that it represents a genie (spirit) which guarded part of the entrance to Cyrus's palace at Parsagarde. It may even be of Cyrus's personal genie or guardian angel.

There was one thing more: the actual tomb.

When viewed nearby, its true size becomes apparent, and the nobility of its lines, the symmetry of its proportions, and the striking whiteness of the marblelike stone of which it is constructed, come out in full effect. It stands high upon a terraced base, seven steps of which are now visible, and the stones, which compose both the substructure and the tomb, are very massive. The lowest stage of the seven terraced steps is a plinth over two feet high, nearly fifty feet long, and more than forty feet broad.

To the best of our knowledge no masonry was employed; the stones were held together, instead, by massive hinges and clamps, some of which have popped up in the nearby soil. The tomb shows evidence of Persian workmanship, but there are aspects of it which suggest that designers and architects may have been brought from as far away as Turkey.

Like many another visitor, Professor Jackson wished to see the inside of Cyrus's tomb, but, unlike many others, he wanted to measure everything as well.

Parsagadae, a city founded by Cyrus, also became the site of his tomb. The inscription on the side of his tomb *(above)* is written in the three languages of the Persian Empire: Old Persian, Elamite, and Babylonian.

The entrance to the tomb is low and narrow, as the Greek authorities state. The height of the doorway is only 4 foot 2 inches and its width 2 foot 7 inches, and it is necessary to crouch in order to pass through as [the Greek writer] Arrian affirmed. The original door to the vault was probably a heavy stone swinging on pivots . . . but I do not recall seeing the socket-holes.

Crawling through the low entrance, Professor Jackson came to the inside of the great tomb. He found the inner room to be 10 feet, 6 inches long; 7 feet, 7 inches wide; and 7 feet, 11 inches in height. There was no trace of the golden casket in which Cyrus the Great had been laid 2,434 years earlier, but that was expected. Many ancient tombs have been pillaged over the centuries; Cyrus's is no exception.

Professor Jackson found few Persian inscriptions within the tomb, but he knew—from ancient writers—that Cyrus had had these words placed on the outside:

O Man, whomsoever thou art, and whencesoever thou comest (for I know thou wilt come), I am Cyrus, who founded the empire of the Persians. Grudge me not therefore this little earth that covers my body.

The words are no longer there, but the thought remains. Professor Jackson spent some time, deep in thought, in the tomb, and his spirit was cast down, perhaps by the inevitable sense that all things—great or terrible, large or small—come to their end. But he had one more revelation that day.

An instant later the setting sun streamed through the doorway and flooded one corner of the dingy vault with a gorgeous splendor. The image of the *kavaya hvarenah*, the 'Kingly Glory,' or symbol of sovereignty in the Avesta [the words of the prophet Zoroaster] flashed across my mind. In ancient times a reflection of this same divine light was believed to shed a halo about the person of the King of Kings. Its sacred majesty was shining this instant from heaven around the tomb of Cyrus and made it seem too hallowed to remain.

Coming out of the tomb, Professor Jackson mounted his horse and rode off as the sun disappeared above the Plain of Murghab. He was neither the first nor the last person to marvel on the majesty of Cyrus, King of Kings, who had created the first world state, and whose tomb still remains for travelers to see.

2

Powers of Light; Powers of Darkness

THERE IS NO AUTHENTICATED IMAGE OF CYRUS THE GREAT, BUT WE imagine him tall, handsome, and dark-haired, for that is how the Aryan peoples liked their leaders.

We have no definite date for Cyrus's birth, but we suspect he was born sometime between 590 and 580 B.C., which would have made him either 20 or 30 at the time he took the Persian throne.

Even Cyrus's religious beliefs—so important to ancient world leaders—are uncertain. He may have been a follower of the prophet Zoroaster, or he may have been a worshipper of the Persian gods and goddesses.

One thing we can say for certain: Cyrus was one of the greatest of ancient world conquerors and one of the most clever of ancient world rulers. He was one of those few men who combined great battlefield tactics with astute diplomacy. Even today, Iranians know him as *The Shepherd*, founder of their nation, symbol of their national consciousness.

THE NOBLE PRINCE

Cyrus was the son of King Cambyses of the Persians, who was himself son of King Cyrus I. To avoid confusing the grandfather and grandson, we will call them Cyrus I (the grandfather) and Cyrus the Great (the grandson).

Cyrus's mother may have been Princess Mandane of the kingdom of the Medes, but this has yet to be conclusively demonstrated; our best source is that of Herodotus, the Greek historian, who said it was so. If true, this means that Cyrus had a lineage that was doubly royal, and that there was some chance he might have peaceably inherited two kingdoms. But the Persians were very much the junior members in their partnership with the Medes, and it is unlikely that the Median nobles would have allowed a Persian to rule them—at least not without a fight.

Cyrus was a Persian, first and foremost, but he was also an Aryan. The word *Aryan* has been misused and abused for nearly a century. Most people associate the word with the absurd racial fantasies of Adolph Hitler and his Nazi followers, but Aryan originally meant "noble." The Aryans were not a race, but a group of peoples, who shared many ethnic similarities. Originally they lived somewhere in the highlands where Iran and Afghanistan meet, but sometime around 1500 B.C. (we cannot be more precise) they began a series of migrations that took them as far as Denmark, Germany, Hungary, northern Greece, northern Turkey, all of Iran, and parts of Afghanistan, Pakistan, and even northern India. This was one of the great migrations of human history, and it is little known to us today because the Aryans left no written records. Archaeologists have found enough traces of pottery and fragments of wagon wheels to suggest that the Aryans were a highly mobile, nomadic people, but that is about all we know.

Everywhere they went, the Aryans met other, more settled peoples. The natives of Pakistan and northern India were displaced (we believe) and the Aryans who moved into northern Greece may have become the ancestors of those who later founded Athens, Corinth, and Sparta. Wherever they went, the Aryans brought with them a simple but intense code of ethics; one of their mainstays was a belief in the power of speech. To an Aryan, telling a lie was one of the worst things a person could do; it limited his or her development as a human being, and it contributed to the forces of darkness, rather than to those of light.

Sometime after the great migrations, perhaps around 1200 B.C., there arose a prophet of singular ability, a man who would help to shape the spiritual future of millions of people. His name was Zoroaster, which means "rich in camels"; the more precise translation is that he was effective, good at handling such beasts.

Little is known of Zoroaster's early years, but we suspect he lived in troubled times. The Aryans had been a peaceful people (at least so he believed) in past days, and now they had become more violent, with many rustling other people's cattle instead of tending to their own. Zoroaster believed it his job to find a solution to this problem—to help make his people more peaceful—but his method would be spiritual rather than material.

One day when he was in his twenties, Zoroaster had a profound vision that changed the rest of his life. While standing near a river or stream (Aryans valued pure water almost as much as they did the pure spoken word), Zoroaster was greeted by a divine being who, along with 10 others, called the

Zoroastrianism was founded by its namesake, Zoro-aster, whose story is similar to that of Moses in the Christian Bible. After meeting with Ahuramazda, the great god constantly in battle with the god of dark-ness, Zoroaster began to preach and convert Persian peoples to this new religion.

"11 Immortals," brought him to the presence of the great god Ahuramazda. This bright shining being was almost too much to look upon, for there was so much radiant peace and power emanating from him. But Zoroaster, like the Hebrew prophet Moses at the burning bush, stayed long enough for instruction about what his teaching should be.

All powers in the universe, Ahuramazda said, were involved in a great and terrible war, one that pitted the forces of light against those of darkness. All human beings, whether they knew it or not, were involved in the great conflict. Everyone's actions, whether they were human or divine, contributed to the growth of the powers of light and truth or those of darkness and deception (Zoroaster later called the powers of darkness "the Big Lie"). This was a great responsibility for humans; they must awake to their choices, and choose the side of light.

No one would argue with that—at least not if he or she saw the beauty and power of the god of light. But Zoroaster faced problems similar to those later faced by Moses: how to convince his people that the vision was genuine?

Many years passed before Zoroaster made his first convert. Happily it turned out to be a local king, probably in what is now Afghanistan. Zoroaster lived peacefully for many years, under the king's protection, but when he sallied forth once more to convert others, he was killed. Many people have claimed to know where his grave is, but these claims have never been authenticated.

Zoroaster was not a monotheist like Moses. He did not say that Ahuramazda was the one and only god; rather, he said that Ahuramazda was in perpetual warfare with the god of darkness and that humans must contribute to that struggle. But Zoroaster was similar to Moses in this way; he preached of an ethical god, one who would make and keep promises, and one upon whose word humans could rely. This was not true of most of the deities of the Middle Eastern world at the time.

Centuries passed, and Cyrus was born.

YOUNG CYRUS

As mentioned above, Cyrus was probably born between 590 and 580 B.C. Of course, he and his fellow Persians did not use the term *Before Christ* (B.C.); that calendar system would not appear for centuries. Instead, they probably reckoned time by the years which had passed since Cambyses, Cyrus's father, had come to the throne. Because Babylon was the greatest power of the ancient world, they may also have reckoned time by the reign of King Nebuchadnezzar of Babylon; what we call 590 B.C. was year 16 of Nebuchadnezzar's reign.

Cyrus and the Persians of that time did not write; like most Aryans, they were devotees of the spoken word, not the written one. Happily, we have the writings of two Greek historians, both of whom were interested in Cyrus.

Herodotus, a Greek who lived about a century after Cyrus, wrote that Cyrus was the son of Cambyses (of which we are sure) and of Princess Mandane of the Medes (here we are on uncertain ground). According to Herodotus, Cyrus was a baby at the court of the kingdom of the Medes, when his grandfather, King Astyages, had a disturbing dream. In this dream Astyages saw a river flow from the stomach of his daughter, Princess Mandane, a river that eventually overflowed to encompass all Asia. Upset and confused, King Astyages summoned his chief soothsayers who said his grandson by Mandane would eventually become the conqueror of all Asia, and would entirely overshadow his grandfather.

Such an outcome was not at all desirable and King Astyages decided the baby must die. Rather than do such a horrid deed himself, the king handed the child to one of his most trusted generals, telling him what to do. Rather than risk the divine

Herodotus and Xenephon

One of the most important questions historians ask is: *How* do we know it? We know, for example, that the Roman Republic changed, over many years, into the Roman Empire, but what are our sources?

Our knowledge of Cyrus the Great comes from a number of sources, but most of them are Greek or Hebrew or Babylonian—almost none of them are directly Persian. Two of our best sources, complete with frailties and misconceptions, are the writings of Herodotus and Xenephon.

Born in about 486 B.C. on the west coast of what is now Turkey, Herodotus grew up a subject of Xerxes I, King of Kings. After many years of travel, and of collecting stories told by others, Herodotus composed his magnificent *The Histories*. Divided into nine chapters are the stories of the Persians, Greeks, Egyptians, and Babylonians, with special emphasis given to the Greco-Persian wars. Herodotus was a Greek patriot, to be sure, but he cared about other peoples as well, and he was interested in finding the truth. Though his stories are uneven—a mixture of fable, fancy, and fact—he deserves the title of Father of History.

Born in Athens in about 450 B.C., Xenephon was an Athenian patriot who, like many leaders of his time, was ostracized—this meant a term of political exile from his home city. Perhaps during this exile, Xenephon came to admire the rival city-state of Sparta for the men it produced. After serving in an army of Greek mercenaries for Cyrus III (also known as Cyrus the Younger), Xenephon wrote a number of books on military tactics and on good and evil in society. He seems to have transferred his admiration of the Spartans to his book on Cyrus the Great, which is called the *Cyropedia* ("The Education of Cyrus"). Some people today call it the first historical novel, for Xenephon clearly invented conversation and tone; even so, the *Cyropedia* is an important source for understanding both Cyrus the Great and Persia and for understanding Xenephon and the Greeks of his time—a century and a half later.

retribution that would surely follow such an evil deed, the general handed the baby to a local shepherd, commanding him to lay it on a hillside where wild animals roamed. Lacking the option to "hand off" the terrible task, the shepherd brought the baby home and was considering what to do when his wife made a proposal. She had recently delivered a stillborn child. They could lay that dead infant on the hillside and raise this son of the palace as their own. The suggestion made good sense, and the shepherd couple raised Cyrus to the age of 10.

As he grew, Cyrus showed signs of a generous disposition, one well suited for leadership. Once, the other children elected him "king" for a day and allowed him to be the boss over them. One of the children, the son of an important nobleman, was distressed both that he had not been selected and that Cyrus gave him orders. Telling his father, this boy soon had Cyrus brought to the palace before King Astyages.

Old and cruel he might be, but Astyages was not blind. He saw the family resemblance at once, and, hearing the story of how this boy had handled the others so adroitly, he realized this was the grandson he had once tried to have killed. Before telling Cyrus the truth, Astyages summoned his counselors and put the matter to them, with the additional information. Confounded they were, at first, but they came up with a clever answer. Cyrus had fulfilled the prophecy of Astyages's dream; he had already been "king" for a day, elected by his fellows. There was nothing more to fear.

Whether he agreed with his counselors (or thought them a bunch of dissemblers) King Astyages did not try to harm Cyrus this time. Instead he sent him home to his true parents, Cambyses and Mandane, to learn the arts of Persian manhood. But the story does have a grisly ending. King Astyages wanted to teach his favored general, who had failed him, a lesson, and the general's punishment—10 years after he was supposed to kill the baby—was to have the head of his own son served up on a dinner plate!

Herodotus, a Greek who was possibly the world's first historian, documented the important events of the Persian Empire during the rule of Cyrus and his descendants. Despite being born almost a century after Cyrus, Herodotus gathered information from Persians to describe the reign of Cyrus the Great in his book *The Histories.*

THE MORAL

One does not have to take this story at face value in order for it to have meaning. Herodotus was a great historian, but he often mixed fancy and fiction with fact and truth. The fact that we suspect the story is full of exaggeration should not lead us to reject the kernels of fact which may lie within.

Very likely Cyrus was not raised by shepherds, and very likely his grandfather King Astyages did not seek to have him killed. But it is quite possible that Cyrus spent some time as a boy at the court of the Medes, and even possible that he spent some time with local shepherds, for both Persians and Medes believed it was necessary to toughen people up. They were Aryans, who had found their way under the sun, stars, and moon for untold generations; they did not wish their children to be housebound.

Whether or not Mandane was his mother, and whether or not his grandfather was a vile man who would try to have a child killed, young Cyrus was indeed alive and well. He grew up at the court of the Persians, the son of their king, but he would have much work to do before he could fulfill any sort of prophecy, especially one which claimed he would be master of all Asia. No one had done that in human history, and no one would do it again until the time of Alexander the Great.

3

The World Cyrus Knew

THE WORLD CYRUS ENTERED WAS ALREADY OLD, IN THAT HUMANS HAD lived in settled areas of the Middle East for well over 2,000 years. His people, the Aryans, had long been an exception to the rule; they had been nomads for untold generations, but that was soon to change.

THE SEMITES

Today the term *Semite* has taken on a different meaning. People say a person is acting anti-Semitic when they mean he or she is acting anti-Jewish or anti-Israeli. But the original meaning of Semite is the many peoples who lived in the Middle East before the Aryans arrived, and who were more often farmers than hunter-gatherers. Aryans and Semites—the boundary between them was rather close to what is now the boundary between Iran and Iraq—could tell each other apart, both through physical characteristics (the Aryans had lighter hair and facial coloring) and through ethnic attitudes.

THE GREAT POWERS OF THE MIDDLE EAST

Most of the great powers around 600 B.C. were Semitic. The time of the Aryans had not yet come. Egypt, secure behind its desert boundaries, still remained potentially the most powerful of all Middle Eastern kingdoms. No other land had for so long maintained an unbroken series of traditions; no other nation had so large a population on which to draw. But Egypt in 600 B.C. was not the Egypt of 1,000 years or even of 300 years earlier. It was a great power that tended to act defensively and reflexively, rather than aggressively. The reasons for this change were multiple, but it is safe to say that Egypt did not threaten its neighbors in 600 B.C., at least not the way it had in the past.

The greatest power of the day was centered in Babylon on the Euphrates River. First settled around 2100 B.C., Babylon had long been an important city, but its population and power had faded between 1000 and 700 B.C., only to revive in a very strong way in approximately 620 B.C. Nebuchadnezzar, its best-known monarch, had become king in 605 B.C. and immediately inaugurated a series of military campaigns and building programs. It was during his long reign that the Hanging Gardens of Babylon became famous, and it was through his insistence that the great walls of Babylon were built to secure the city. Nebuchadnezzar was ambitious for Babylon in all sorts of ways; he built on the contributions of earlier Babylonians, and made his empire the most powerful of the time.

When Nebuchadnezzar looked east he saw the growing power of the Aryan tribes, the Persians and the Medes most especially. He did not fear they would attack his kingdom, but

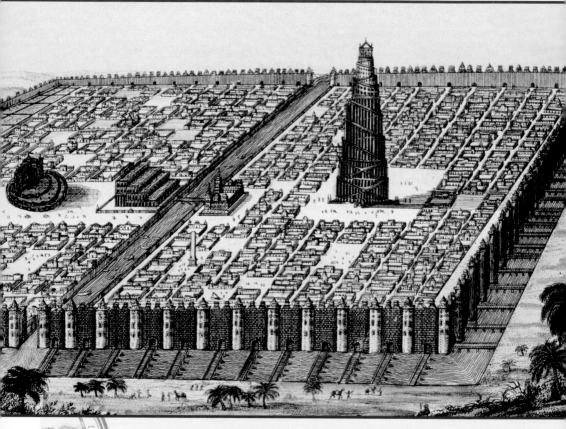

One of the most amazing ancient cities, Babylon's marvels and wonders included the Hanging Gardens and two walls to secure the city from invaders. Cyrus's desire to conquer certain regions led to his liberation of many people who had helped build Babylon.

he saw that they stood in the way of any eastward expansion. When he looked west, Nebuchadnezzar saw the small kingdoms of Judah and Phoenicia. These small sets of lands seemed ripe for the picking. But Nebuchadnezzar was also aware of the growing power of Lydia, which was situated to his northwest.

The Lydian kingdom, based in what is now central and western Turkey, had been a small-time power just a hundred years earlier, but the discovery of gold and silver mines in the Turkish hills had changed everything. Lydia had become the richest of all Middle Eastern kingdoms; its leaders were among the first anywhere to have their image stamped on coins. Lydia had neither the vast population of Egypt nor the great land space of Babylon, but its wealth and the skill of its cavalry (Lydian horsemen were considered the best of the time) suggested it was a power on the rise.

Nebuchadnezzar stayed on good terms with Lydia. He was a perennial foe of Egypt, but the two nations were at peace about the time Cyrus was born. If Nebuchadnezzar had one great ambition, one area which he wanted to conquer, it was the eastern rim of the Mediterranean Sea, the homeland of the Hebrews and Phoenicians.

SMALL KINGDOMS

We know more about the ancient Hebrews than about most other ancient world peoples, largely because of the writings in the Old Testament. Many parts of the Hebrew Bible have been called into question—often with good reason—but no other people left such a detailed record of their names, their kings, and their prophets. Occasionally, archaeology is able to prove or disprove something that is written in the Bible; such is the case with the Hebrew King Jehu, who prostrated himself and offered tribute to the king of Assyria. This episode in the Book of Kings was thoroughly validated when an ancient stela (an inscribed stone), depicting the event, was discovered. Today it is housed with the British Museum in London.

Other things described in the Old Testament have come under scrutiny and been found wanting. Although many Hebrews may have gone to Egypt, and been enslaved, the archaeological record does not yet indicate the mass Exodus described in the Bible. Historians are reasonably confident, however, that

David was the first major king of the Hebrews, and that the temple, located on the extreme eastern side of Jerusalem, was built in the reign of his son, King David. That is where we pick up our story of the Hebrews (they are called Jews after the return from Babylon).

The Hebrews were united in the time of King Solomon, but later they broke into two distinct groups: the kingdom of Israel in the north and the kingdom of Judah in the south (including Jerusalem). During the ninth and eighth centuries B.C., the

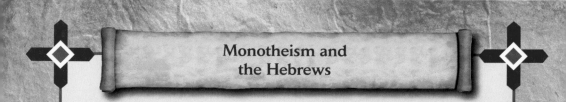

Monotheism and the Hebrews

The ancient Hebrews may not have been the first or only monotheists, but they are the only ones who left a record of the progression of their beliefs. The Old Testament takes the reader from the time of Abraham, Sarah, and Isaac all the way to the time of Christ.

The Hebrews were a Semitic people whose origins were in what is now southeastern Iraq; the Old Testament says that Abraham left the city of Ur to found a new place for his tribe in what is now Israel. There was no racial or ethnic difference between the ancient Hebrews and the ancient Babylonians; the difference was religious and cultural.

Abraham was the world's first known monotheist, meaning that he worshipped one God and disdained or rejected all others. His God was *Yahweh*, which, in ancient Hebrew, means "he causes [it] to be." This means that Yahweh was a supernatural god, one whose powers were above nature, while most of the gods and goddesses of that time were associated with nature: the god of thunder or the goddess of flowing water, for example.

Hebrews came under increasing attack from their neighbors, the Assyrians most of all. In 722 B.C., the northern kingdom of Israel was destroyed by the Assyrians; this was the beginning of the story of the "Ten Lost Tribes" of Israel, which has continued down to our present day. The kingdom of Judah remained, but it lived on borrowed time.

At the beginning of the sixth century B.C., close to the time of Cyrus's birth, the southern kingdom of Judah was troubled by protests, rebellions, and concerns over waning

Abraham and his wife Sarah had a son, even though they were greatly advanced in age (this miracle came from Yahweh). When the boy was five or six, Yahweh commanded Abraham to show his obedience by using the child as a sacrifice, as one might offer a sheep, ram, or calf. Abraham was horrified, but the more he rationalized it, the more he came to understand that since God had given him this great gift of a son, God could call it back. Abraham took Isaac to Mount Moriah (in what is now Jerusalem) and prepared to sacrifice his son to Yahweh.

At a critical moment, just when the boy had realized he was to be the sacrifice, an angel descended and told Abraham not to harm the child, that Yahweh had seen the quality of his faith, and that all was well. Abraham lived a good many years longer and, through his son Isaac, was the father of the ancient Hebrews.

One can be forgiven for asking: What kind of god was this? Yahweh seems, to our modern eyes, to be a harsh and unforgiving deity. But that should not surprise us. Abraham's relationship with Yahweh took place at a time when all the gods and goddesses demanded sacrifice and propitiation from their believers. Abraham and the early Hebrews turned a major corner when they became monotheists, but they did not abandon all the traditions of their time.

morality. The prophet Jeremiah, whose *Lamentations* form an important part of the Old Testament, cried out that the people of Judah had gone back on their agreement with Yahweh, and that the kingdom would soon be destroyed. "Look not to help from military strength," Jeremiah said, "for when the people have lost their morals, God will surely bring them low."

It seemed that King Nebuchadnezzar was God's instrument.

In 597 B.C., Nebuchadnezzar brought the Babylonian army right up to the gates of Jerusalem. King Jehoiakim had not sent the proper tribute to Babylon (as King Jehu had done with the Assyrians long ago). Nebuchadnezzar subdued the city and took both the king and about 5,000 Hebrews, most of them leading merchants and politicians, into captivity in Babylon. Thus began what the Hebrews called the Babylonian Captivity; the expression has since been used to describe any long form of exile or punishment.

The prophet Jeremiah, who had foreseen this disaster, spoke: "For who shall have pity on thee, O Jerusalem? Or who shall bemoan thee? Or who shall go to pray for thy peace? Thou hast forsaken me, saith the Lord, thou art gone backward; and I will stretch out my hand against thee, and I will destroy thee. I am weary of entertaining thee." (Jeremiah 15:5–6)

Things were about to become even worse.

Nebuchadnezzar saw that the kingdom of Judah and the kingdom of Phoenicia, both of them small powers, were the keys to the eastern side of the Mediterranean Sea. He laid siege to the major Phoenician cities, bringing down all except the city of Tyre, which lay about half a mile off shore, and was impregnable against his assaults. In 587 B.C., just a decade after his first attack, Nebuchadnezzar came against Jerusalem once more, for the puppet king he had installed there had proved no better than the previous Hebrew one. This time Nebuchadnezzar took nearly all the population as captives; he had his men destroy the city itself, including the glorious temple built in the time of King Solomon.

The Babylonian king Nebuchadnezzar flattened Jerusalem as predicted by the prophet Jeremiah, seen *(above)* sitting in the middle of the battle. After removing some of the city's most important people, Nebuchadnezzar returned to Jerusalem nearly a decade later and destroyed the Temple of Solomon, one of the Hebrews' most meaningful religious sites.

This was the single greatest blow, for the people of Judah venerated the temple, which was their connection to the days of Solomon and David (when the building was completed) as well as to the time of Abraham. The Hebrews believed that this was where he had taken his only son, Isaac, when he planned to sacrifice him to Yahweh.

The kingdom of Judah lay in ruins after the departure of Nebuchadnezzar. He valued its land more as a boundary between Egypt and himself than for its own sake, and the vineyards of what is now southern Israel were laid waste. Thousands of Hebrews went to Babylon as captives, where they were not treated badly. Nebuchadnezzar had them live in a certain section of Babylon (one could call this the first ghetto), but the Hebrew captives were able to work their trades and sell their wares. Babylonian captivity was not nearly as harsh as the Egyptian captivity described in the *Book of Exodus,* but that did not change the basic formula: The Hebrews were captives, dispossessed of their lands.

THE ECLIPSE

At about the same time Nebuchadnezzar went to war with Judah and Phoenicia, the Medians and Lydians went to war with each other.

As mentioned above, the kingdom of Lydia was the richest of all ancient lands. The kingdom of Media, which was in what is now northern Iran and Iraq, was composed of Aryan peoples who had wandered the high plateau for untold generations before settling into their capital city of Ecbatana (in present-day western Iran). The two nations went to war in about 590 B.C., fighting for possession of the mountainous areas of eastern Turkey (where many Kurds live today).

The Greek historian Herodotus tells us that in the sixth year of the war the two peoples were involved in a great battle, which might have determined the war's outcome, when there was a sudden eclipse of the sun. The natural event terrified both peoples, making them think that the gods and goddesses were against this war. Lydia and Media quickly came to peace, establishing the Halys River in central Turkey as their boundary.

Herodotus goes on to say that the eclipse had been predicted by the Greek scientist Thales, who lived in Miletus, in what is now western Turkey. Because of the circumstances described and because of the calculations of modern science, we are now quite confident in saying that the Battle of the Eclipse, as it is called, took place in May 585 B.C. This is one of the first precise dates from ancient history of which we are certain, and we can thank both the Babylonian astronomers for their accurate records and Herodotus for telling the story.

This world, in which polytheism predominated but where monotheism was on the rise, and where science alternated with fantasy, was the one Cyrus knew. It was not the same world he would leave behind.

4

From Prince to King

CYRUS WAS A PRINCE—OF THAT WE ARE SURE—BUT NOT ONE IN THE WAY we envision today. There were few trappings of office, and he may have lived a very athletic and rugged life in his youth, as did most Persians of that time.

Persia corresponds roughly to the province of Fars in southwestern Iran today. This is a high, dry land, where mountains abound, but they are spread out over the land, not concentrated, so they are not a massive chain like the Rocky Mountains, for example. Even so, southwestern Iran remains a land of prophecy and inspiration, for the people of these highlands think—and thought—themselves superior to all others. The rivalry between mountain people and lowland ones was one of the most consistent themes of ancient history, with many battles and wars fought between the two. Let Herodotus explain how the Persians thought of themselves:

> When they meet each other in the streets, you may know if the persons meetings are of equal rank by the following token; if they are, instead of speaking, they kiss each other on the lips. . . . Of nations, they honor most their nearest neighbors, whom they esteem next to themselves; those who live beyond these they honor in the second degree; and so with the remainder, the further they are removed, the less the esteem in which they hold them. The reason is, that they look upon themselves as very greatly superior in all respects to the rest of mankind.

Part of this feeling of superiority came from their geographic location. Born and bred to the severe weather of the mountains, Persians thought less of people who lived in easier, gentler climates. Herodotus went on to describe their religion:

> They have no images of the gods, no temples nor altars, and consider the use of them a sign of folly. This comes, I think, from their not believing the gods to have the same nature with men, as the Greeks imagine. Their wont, however, is to ascend the summits of the loftiest mountains, and there to offer sacrifice.

It makes sense that a people proud of their mountain heritage would go up lofty peaks to sacrifice to the gods, but the Persians were also keen on fire and water, which they saw as natural forces that embodied the will and power of the gods. Herodotus labored a good deal to explain how fastidious the Persians were, how they would never defile a stream or any running water, which they held sacred.

Sadly, we have very few records from the Persians themselves. One of the few is an emblem that shows King Cyrus I,

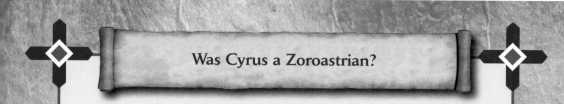

Was Cyrus a Zoroastrian?

This is one of the most interesting, and perplexing, of all questions about Cyrus the Great. We know, generally speaking, the order and succession of his conquests, and we know the type of government he set up after his victories. His religion remains a matter of conjecture.

For some time historians assumed Cyrus was a Zoroastrian because they believed that the great king and the great prophet lived at about the same time; this theory also assumes that the new religion was part of what aided Cyrus in his many conquests. But recent textual deconstruction by leading scholars assures us that the prophet Zoroaster lived long before Cyrus, perhaps about the same time as Moses, and that being a Zoroastrian would not have assisted Cyrus in his campaigns.

Nineteenth-century archaeologists also pointed to the magnificent mountain carvings at Behistun, Iran. This is not a set of carvings of Cyrus, or of his times, but of his son-in-law Darius, who became King of Kings around 521 B.C., nine years after Cyrus's death. Darius had the inscriptions written in three different languages, which is, in part, how we are now able to interpret old Persian writing. Darius referred frequently to the Lord Ahuramazda, chief of all the gods, and said that it was because of Ahuramazda that Darius had been able to achieve great things. Why, historians ask, did not Cyrus write something similar? Does this suggest he was *not* a Zoroastrian?

The foremost scholar of Zoroastrianism, Mary Boyce (who died in 2006), was convinced from her research that Cyrus and his immediate family were followers of the prophet Zoroaster. She gave both anecdotal and circumstantial evidence, including the fact that Cyrus named one of his daughters, Atossa, for a leading character in the story of Zoroaster. But other scholars disagreed, and the controversy continued.

grandfather of Cyrus the Great, hunting on horseback. That accords with what we know of the Persians, an Aryan people, who loved open spaces and the chase.

XENEPHON'S CYRUS

It would be remiss of us not to describe something of what Xenephon wrote about Cyrus the Great. Born a century and a half after Cyrus, and a good 50 years after Herodotus, Xenephon was an Athenian who, exiled from his home city, went on a number of campaigns, including one that penetrated the Persian Empire of that time (about 400 B.C.). Xenephon greatly admired the Persian king he served (a descendant of Cyrus), and the more he traveled the more he became enamored of the original Cyrus. Xenephon's *The Education of Cyrus* is one of the few ancient texts, along with Herodotus, that has come down to us little changed over the centuries; reading, we feel as if we are there and that the voice of Xenephon can be heard. Let us listen to a conversation between Cyrus and his father King Cambyses:

> There is no shorter road, my son, than really to be wise in those things in which you wish to seem wise; and when you examine concrete instances, you will realize that what I say is true. For example, if you wish to seem to be a good farmer when you are not, or a good rider, doctor, flute-player, or anything else that you are not, just think of how many schemes you must invent to keep up your pretensions. And even if you should persuade any number of people to praise you, in order to give yourself a reputation, and if you should procure a fine outfit for each of your professions, you would soon be found to have practiced deception; and not long after, when you were giving an exhibition of your skill, you would be shown up and convicted, too, as an imposter.

Xenophon *(above)* was a mercenary fighting with Cyrus the Younger against the Persians when he came to admire Cyrus the Great. After Cyrus the Younger was defeated in Persia, Xenophon began his retirement as a writer. One of his books was written about the life of Cyrus the Great.

The basic theme of this discourse resounds in the words of Abraham Lincoln, uttered more than 2,000 years later: "You can fool some of the people all of the time, and all of the people some of the time, but you can't fool all of the people all of the time." But Xenephon wrote this long before Lincoln expressed the idea, and, given that Lincoln was a voracious reader, it's possible he obtained part of the idea from reading Xenephon.

Xenephon portrays King Cambyses as a wise, though old and tired, man, and Cyrus as a vigorous, excitable young one. This was a staple of Greek literature, for the Greeks believed a man could become a full man only by being among men, especially those older than he. Whether Cyrus really enjoyed such a close relationship with his father is not known; there are suggestions that King Cambyses had to be a very skillful diplomat, for he was king of Persia at a time when that small kingdom could have been swallowed up by any of the major powers, including Babylonia and Media.

Whether Cyrus was as close to his father as Xenephon suggests or not, the matter became academic when King Cambyses died in 559 B.C. Cyrus was now king of Persia.

FIRST DECISIONS

Cyrus took the Persian throne at about the same time that Nabonidus became king of Babylon and Croesus became king of Lydia. The lives and reigns of the three kings would be interconnected.

As discussed in Chapter 1, it is impossible for us to say whether Cyrus was a grandson of King Astyages of Media, but we are certain that conflict began between the two almost as soon as Cyrus ascended the Persian throne. Persians and Medes were both Aryan people, cousins in fact, and they had got along well for the past 50 years, but that was due in part to the submission shown by Persian leaders Cyrus I and Cambyses I. Now there was a young man on the Persian throne (we estimate Cyrus was somewhere between 20 and 30 at the time). Herodotus described the situation at the time of Cyrus's accession:

> The Persian nation is made up of many tribes. Those which
> Cyrus assembled and persuaded to revolt from the Medes,

Parsagadae, located in Iran, was the site of Cyrus the Great's victory against King Astyages, the ruler of Medes. Years after this arduous fight, Cyrus declared the battleground to be the location of his new palace and the city of Persia.

were the principal ones on which all the others are dependent. These are the Parsagadae, the Maraphians, and the Maspians, of whom the Parsagadae are the noblest. The Achaemenids, from which spring all the Persian kings, is one of their clans. The rest of the Persian tribes are the following: the Panthilaeans, the Derusians, the Germanians, who are engaged in husbandry, the Daans, the Mardians, the Dropicans, and the Sagartians, who are nomads.

Historians are grateful to Herodotus for this list because no Persian writing from that time described and named the different tribes. Once they became world conquerors, the different tribes were known simply as Persians.

Cyrus received messengers from King Astyages demanding he send tokens of submission to the court of the Medes at the city of Ecbatana; the traditional tokens were bowls of earth and water, showing that the smaller, less powerful, king received all that he held by the good grace of the more important one. But Cyrus did not send the symbols of submission, and when another messenger arrived to say that King Astyages wanted to see him, Cyrus retorted that Astyages would see him sooner than he wished.

CYRUS'S FIRST WAR

Cyrus's reign and career would be intimately connected with warfare, but the first—and in some ways the most important— of his conflicts was with the Medes. Between 555 and 551 B.C., he fought a series of battles against the generals of King Astyages and was defeated as often as he was victorious. The climactic battle, according to Persian tradition, took place in an especially beautiful section of Persia, a big bowl of land in a high plateau that the natives call Murghab. There, the Persians and the Medes fought all day, while the Persian women stood on one of the nearby heights to call out in support of their men. The battle was long and hard but Cyrus eventually prevailed, and this time he took King Astyages prisoner, meaning the war was over. Just a few years later, Cyrus chose the battle site to be the location for his palace and ceremonial capital; it is called Parsagadae today.

One more time we have to admit that we do not know if Cyrus and Astyages were truly blood kin, as some historians tell us. But whether they were or not, Cyrus showed magnanimity in victory; he not only allowed Astyages to live, but he treated him well and kept him as an honored prisoner for the rest of his life. If this shows Cyrus had a generous nature—and many sources attest to it—it also indicates he was wise, for kings and queens generally do not kill other royalty, lest the common people start to think it a commonplace event.

By about 550 B.C., Cyrus had become king of the Medes as well as of the Persians. His kingdom, which one could almost call an empire, now stretched through virtually all of what is modern-day Iran and the northern part of what is now Iraq. This meant the Lydians, under King Croesus, had become his close neighbors.

CHAPTER

5

Toward the Setting Sun

AS DESCRIBED IN CHAPTER THREE, THE LYDIANS AND THE MEDIANS HAD been foes, fighting a six-year war at about the time when Cyrus was born. The Battle of the Eclipse had brought that war to an end, and there had been peace along the Halys River ever since.

CROESUS VERSUS CYRUS

By about 548 B.C., King Croesus had become very nervous about Cyrus's growing strength. Croesus was the richest monarch of his day, and Lydia was in no danger from Cyrus's Persians, partly because of the long distances to be covered. Lydia was based in what is now central and western Turkey, which

51

were difficult for Cyrus to reach. But Croesus became the aggressor, starting a war in 547 B.C.

Before starting the conflict, Croesus sent messengers to each of the seven leading oracles of which he had knowledge. There were two or three in Turkey, two or three in Greece, and another in far-off Africa, but Croesus sent letters to them all. Each of his messengers was ordered to pose the same question to the oracles: What is King Croesus doing right now? To make the matter more certain, Croesus ordered his messengers to ask the question on the one-hundredth day after they left Sardis, capital of Lydia.

Each of the seven major oracles returned an answer, but only one, the Oracle of the god Apollo at Delphi, got it right. The answer of the Pythoness, a woman who spoke for Apollo, was:

> I can count the sands, and I can measure the ocean. I have ears for the silent, and know what the dumb man meaneth; Lo! On my sense there striketh the smell of a shell-covered tortoise, Boiling now on a fire, with the flesh of a lamb, in a cauldron,—Brass is the vessel below, and brass the cover above it.

Whether the Pythoness was "tipped off" or not, we shall never know; but the Oracle of Apollo had the right answer; King Croesus had made a lamb-and-tortoise stew on the one-hundredth day after his messengers left Sardis.

Overjoyed with the accuracy of this oracle, King Croesus sent a series of major gifts to Delphi. There were pots of gold and plates of silver, and, above all else, a gold statue of a lion. Historians later doubted that Croesus was so magnanimous, but a series of archaeological discoveries in the 1930s verified that here Herodotus was indeed correct. Not long after sending his gifts, Croesus also sent a second major question to the Oracle of Apollo. This time his query was: What would happen if he crossed the Halys River to start a war with Cyrus

King Croesus, ruler of Lydia, gained vast wealth as he conquered neighboring lands. He hoarded his treasure in Sardis, the capital, and displayed it for visitors like Solon, a Greek statesman *(above)*. Other treasures were kept in Delphi, the temple home of the Greek god Apollo and the famed oracle, who provided Croesus with veiled predictions.

and the Persians? The answer came back, quick as before: If Cyrus crossed the River Halys, he would destroy a great empire. Thinking this must surely mean that Cyrus and Persia would fall, Croesus laid his plans for the summer of 547 B.C.

Cyrus must have had spies in Lydia, for he was not taken unawares. In the spring of 547 B.C., he moved north-by-northwest, coming close to—but not attacking—the Babylonian fortifications along the Tigris River. Leaving that area, he continued northwest, and came to what is now the Turkish-Iraqi border with his very sizeable army (we do not know the number of his men, but we trust Herodotus when he assures us that Cyrus had much the larger force than Croesus).

Numbers do not tell the whole story, of course, and the Lydian cavalry was famed as the best of its day. Moreover, Cyrus had hired a large number of Greek and Egyptian mercenaries, so his was a multinational army; the same could be said of Cyrus, though most of his men were Aryans at least, and their languages were close enough that they did not need interpreters.

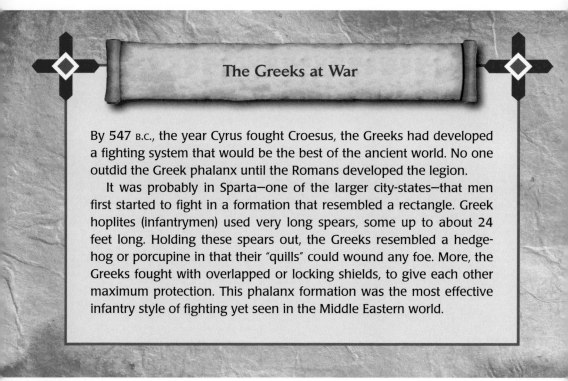

The Greeks at War

By 547 B.C., the year Cyrus fought Croesus, the Greeks had developed a fighting system that would be the best of the ancient world. No one outdid the Greek phalanx until the Romans developed the legion.

It was probably in Sparta—one of the larger city-states—that men first started to fight in a formation that resembled a rectangle. Greek hoplites (infantrymen) used very long spears, some up to about 24 feet long. Holding these spears out, the Greeks resembled a hedgehog or porcupine in that their "quills" could wound any foe. More, the Greeks fought with overlapped or locking shields, to give each other maximum protection. This phalanx formation was the most effective infantry style of fighting yet seen in the Middle Eastern world.

Cyrus and Croesus met on the extreme eastern side of the Cappadocian Plain, in what is now Turkey. The two generals maneuvered and counter-maneuvered for some weeks before coming to grips in a battle that lasted all day. When the Lydian horsemen charged, they carried all before them, but when the Persians drew their bows and released their arrows, even the Lydian cavalry had to withdraw. The battle was a bloody stalemate, with neither side prevailing.

Soon after the battle, Croesus decided it was time to retire for the winter. It was early autumn, but he knew how bare the Cappadocian Plain could be at this time of year. Marching quickly away, he moved by rapid stages to his capital at Sardis, where he released his Greek and Egyptian mercenaries, telling them to return five months hence. So far Croesus had planned well, but he had not reckoned on Cyrus.

The hoplites were all equal; there were few officers; and the men in the phalanx fought as one. This took great coordination and trust on their part, something that could only be developed between men who fought on a basis of equality. There are those who say that the phalanx helped bring about Greek democracy, and others who say that Greek democracy made possible the phalanx. Whichever came first, it is indeed likely that the one fed the other.

Cyrus never met a purely Greek army in battle, and, given his brilliance, we imagine he would have found a way to offset their tactical advantages. But some of his successors, Darius I and Xerxes I most especially, would rue the day they sent their best Persian infantrymen to fight the Greeks.

Whether he obtained his skill from battles in youth, or whether he acquired it slowly as the years passed, Cyrus was now a commander with a fine strategic sense. He had seen how effective the Lydian cavalry was, and he did not wish to wait for the coming spring to fight again, on what would be equal terms. Breaking most, if not all, of the rules of ancient world warfare, Cyrus waited a few days so Croesus had a head start, then quietly followed him across the plains and valleys of central Turkey. So quietly did they move, and so well did they use their scouts, that the Persians followed Croesus all the way to Sardis before he knew they were upon his heels. Just a few days after arriving at his beloved capital city, Croesus found himself besieged.

Croesus knew that his allies and mercenaries would return in the spring, but he was not certain he could hold out that long. A day after Cyrus's arrival, Croesus sent his famed Lydian cavalry into the plain below.

The Lydian horsemen moved rapidly, as was their style, and were about to come to grips with the Persian enemy when they found their horses would go no further. Cyrus had set up a thin screen of camels in front of his own lines.

In the daylong battle in eastern Turkey, Cyrus had noticed that the Lydian horses seemed to dislike both the sight and smell of camels. Bringing along a number of the beasts, Cyrus arranged them in order to throw off the Lydian horses. Forced to dismount, the Lydian cavalrymen proved much less effective as infantrymen, and by sunset Cyrus had chased the Lydian army entirely into Sardis.

Croesus should have been able to hold out for months but Cyrus did not wait that long. As Herodotus tells it, a Mardian (one of the 10 Persian tribes) soldier, walking around the citadel of Sardis, observed a Lydian descending from the height to retrieve a helmet that had fallen. This particular part of the city was weakly defended because its natural defenses were so strong, but Cyrus, once alerted, believed that where a Lydian could go, his Persians could follow. The very next day, Croesus

In his victory against Croesus, Cyrus expanded his empire and gained all the gold and silver of the Lydian civilization, much of which was in the neighborhood of its capital, Sardis.

awoke to learn that fighting had commenced and there were Persians within the walls. The battle was brief and Sardis was taken.

Modern readers may hear this with skepticism. How could Croesus have left a section so poorly defended? How could so small an event as the retrieval of a helmet lead to the capture of one of the important cities of the ancient world? But military history is replete with examples like this one. Take, for example, how the British captured Quebec City in 1759, by using a path up a steep slope the French had not fortified, or how the British failed to capture George Washington and his army in 1776 because of a fog-filled evening. Whether the Mardian and the helmet were indeed the turning point is less important than the fact that Cyrus won and Croesus became his prisoner.

Like King Astyages, who had been captured five years earlier, King Croesus was treated well in captivity. Cyrus kept both men prisoners until the time of their deaths, but he did so in a humane and generous way; Herodotus goes as far as to say that Cyrus used Croesus as an informal advisor and that the former Lydian king showed much wisdom in this new role. Be that as it may, Cyrus now had the gold and silver of Lydia, as well as the capital city of Sardis. By now, he was the greatest commander of his age, bar none; the only conqueror to whom he could properly be compared was King Nebuchadnezzar, who had died about 20 years earlier.

CYRUS AND THE GREEKS

By the spring of 546 B.C., most of what is now Turkey was under Persian control. The major exception was a sliver of land on Turkey's west coast, where a handful of Greek city-states still held out. Some of them sent a delegation to Cyrus, offering to become his allies, but he taunted them by telling the story of the piper who piped to a bunch of fish and was spurned; only after he caught them did they wish to dance for him. Cyrus now wished to complete his conquest by taking all the land that led to the Mediterranean Sea. Given that he was essentially a landsman, one who had never taken to the ocean, we imagine that this was the extent of his ambition in that direction: He had reached the land of the setting sun.

CHAPTER

6

To the
Rising Dawn

CYRUS WAS AT THE TOP OF SUCCESS IN THE YEAR 546 B.C. MOST OF TURKEY was his, and his empire now stretched from Parsagadae in what is now Iran all the way to the Greek city-states that dotted the Turkish coast. But there were always new challenges and challengers to his growing majesty.

Very soon after he conquered Sardis and took the Lydian kingdom, Cyrus was accosted by a deputation from the city-state of Sparta. Cyrus, the Spartans said, should not molest the Greek city-states on the Turkish coast (which was then called Ionia), for they, the Spartans, would not allow it. Full of wrath, Cyrus turned to his advisers and demanded, "Who *are* the Spartans?" He told the deputation that Sparta would soon have plenty to worry about with its own safety; that it should not concern itself with the other Greek states. But Cyrus also included the words, "If I live," in his threat, and this was telling, for though he had come to the throne as a young man, hard years of campaigning were making him an old one. Like many another great conqueror—Napoleon comes to mind—Cyrus was worried about his health.

Perhaps this was why Cyrus left his task uncompleted. Usually he stayed with a conquest from beginning to end, but two years had passed since he had seen Parsagadae, and his Persian governors back home may have been growing restless. Then, too, Cyrus felt fulfilled with his drive to the west and was beginning to think about the east. For these reasons, and perhaps others as well, he headed back home soon after threatening the Spartans. Almost as soon as he left, trouble broke out in the recently conquered areas.

First, the people of Sardis revolted. The Persian garrison was put to the sword, and a new leader emerged, who claimed he would lead the Lydians and the Greeks to freedom.

Cyrus was about 500 miles away when he heard the news. He could not afford to turn back and subdue this revolt himself, so he sent one of his trusted generals back west, with orders to punish the revolt without mercy. This was unusual for Cyrus, but he wanted to make an example of the Lydians and the Greeks.

Cyrus's general quickly retook Sardis, but he found it nearly impossible to track down the man who had masterminded the revolt. While he was still on the man's trail, several of the Greek city-states broke out in open revolt. Suddenly it seemed as if Cyrus's grand conquest of Turkey was in peril.

Herodotus tells us that the people of one Greek city-state put all their goods on a number of ships and sailed off rather than live under Persian rule. Born in Halicarnassus, on the Turkish coast, Herodotus may well have been right about this. The Greeks sailed for Sardinia to establish a colony there.

Cyrus's general, who had been sent to subdue the revolt, died of natural causes, and Cyrus sent another, by the name of

Like the more famous Cyrus Cylinder, the Cylinder of Nabonidus *(above)* tells a long tale about how a king appeases his people and the gods by rebuilding a temple in order to frame his own accomplishments in refurbishing three temples in Babylon.

Harpagus. One by one the Greek city-states were conquered, often by the method of building large earthen mounds that came closer and closer to the city walls. Within a year of being sent to western Turkey, Harpagus had brought most of the area back to Persian rule. But neither he nor Cyrus ever trusted the Greeks again; both seemed to have a premonition that the Greeks would present troubles in the future (as indeed happened, in the time of Darius and Xerxes).

Cyrus made it home sometime in the year 545 B.C. Seldom has a conqueror returned to such a series of festivals and rejoicings. In the 14 years since he had become king of Persia, Cyrus had created the largest land empire seen since the time of the Assyrians, and he had done so without imitating the Assyrians' cruelty. When he looked around, Cyrus saw only one remaining real rival to his greatness: the king of Babylon.

NABONIDUS

As mentioned in Chapter 1, King Nebuchadnezzar, who reigned from 605 to 562 B.C., was the greatest ruling conqueror of his time. When Nebuchadnezzar died, Babylon was very much the greatest Middle Eastern power.

No fewer than three monarchs followed in quick succession. The unsettled state of affairs was concluded when Nabonidus (also called Nabunaid) took the throne in March of 555 B.C.

Controversy surrounded Nabonidus in his lifetime and it has remained with his legacy ever since. Was he an usurper, a high noble who took the throne from the royal family, or was he a grandson of King Nebuchadnezzar, who, because of his matrilineal descent, had not been expected to rise to the throne? The Babylonians themselves seemed a little uncertain about the matter and we moderns are at a loss to discover the truth. What is clear, however, is that Nabonidus, whether he was royal or not, intended to alter some of the Babylonian religious festivals. New

After defeating Croesus in Lydia, Cyrus marched east with his armies, in the direction of modern-day Afghanistan. Cyrus expanded his empire by using his large forces to defeat resistance from the local people.

Year's Day was celebrated in Babylon with an enormous festival, which drew thousands of people from outlying districts; on this day, the Babylonian king was expected to walk slowly up to the statue of the great God Marduk, place his hands in those of the god's statue, and thereby receive an annual blessing for the land. Nabonidus performed the festival during the first few years of his reign, but he then moved, on a temporary basis, to a desert oasis in Arabia, which is now Saudi Arabia. Nabonidus spent most of his time at this oasis, building new statues to the gods; he seemed especially well disposed toward the moon god Sin (some believe his mother was a priestess of Sin).

The Babylonian people were not upset with King Nabonidus but the Babylonian merchants were. They depended on the New Year's festival for much of their annual income, and when the king was not in Babylon, the festival was not performed. Resentment grew as the years passed.

Nabonidus was conscious of Cyrus the Great from an early point in his reign; the Babylonian Chronicle holds tantalizingly brief references both to Cyrus's revolt against Astyages and then his campaign against King Croesus. Nabonidus did not yet fear Cyrus, for Babylon and its surrounding areas were protected by the most elaborate system of fortifications yet seen in the ancient world; even the Assyrians had not built as many walls, towers, and gates as had the Babylonians under Nebuchadnezzar. Cyrus was equally aware of Nabonidus, and, we suspect, was already laying plans for his downfall. But before Cyrus could do anything about the king of Babylon, he had to tend to business in the far east.

BACTRIA AND SOGDIANA

These were the names of what we now call Afghanistan and the southern part of Turkestan. The flatlands south and west of the Oxus River teemed with peoples, many of whom were on the move. Cyrus may even have wished to go east in order to find Aryan-vej, the mythic place where his Aryan ancestors had commenced their many journeys. Herodotus provides us with one of our few contemporary views of the Scythians.

> Oaths among the Scythians are accompanied with the following ceremonies: a large earthen bowl is filled with wine, and the parties to the oath, wounding themselves slightly with a knife or an awl, drop some of their blood into the wine; then they plunge into the mixture a scimitar, some arrows, a battle-axe, and a javelin, all the while repeating prayers; lastly the two contracting parties drink each a draught from the bowl.

Herodotus also described the tombs of Scythian kings, which, he said, were full of ornaments (some of this has been verified by twentieth-century archaeology). The Scythians were certainly different from Persians, Greeks, and others, but there was plenty of contact between the peoples: The great Athenian orator Demosthenes had a Scythian mother.

CYRUS IN THE EAST

We know little about Cyrus's eastward procession. Very likely he and his men navigated their way by keeping the Snow Mountain (present-day Mount Alvand, just outside of Tehran) constantly in view. We imagine that there were few pitched battles along the way, for Cyrus now had a large army, and the peoples he met had very small ones. But the closer he came to Bactria, which is now northern Afghanistan, the more likely it is that he was drawn into skirmishes with the mountain folk, many of whom had never known a conqueror, much less a ruler.

We believe that Cyrus crossed the Oxus River, which flows west into the Aral Sea and that he went even farther, all the way to the Jaxartes River, which was considered the boundary between the civilized and barbarian worlds (of course the difference between "civilized" and "barbarian" is highly relative).

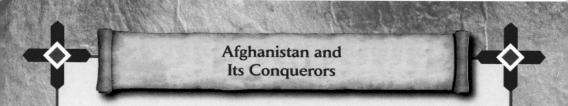

Afghanistan and Its Conquerors

Northern Afghanistan roughly corresponds to what people of the ancient world called Bactria and Sogdiana. We know that Cyrus passed through these areas—though he may deliberately have avoided the highest elevations—and that Alexander came through two centuries later.

Alexander married a Bactrian princess named Roxanne. It is said that he won her by surprising her father, a tribal chieftain, who had dared the Macedonians and Greeks to assail his mountain stronghold (like Cyrus in front of Sardis, Alexander found a way to scale the heights). The tribespeople of northern Afghanistan still remember Alexander today; they call him al-Iskandar al-Akbar (Alexander the Great).

Many other conquerors and would-be conquerors came that way in the nineteenth and twentieth centuries. The British came from India in the south, and were thoroughly defeated in a battle near the Khyber Pass. The Russians came down from the north in 1979, and were humiliated in a war that lasted more than a decade. What, one wonders, makes the Afghanis so fierce?

Perhaps it is from generations of living in isolation from the modern world, and from having no conveniences with which to make life easier. Herodotus and Xenephon both praised the early Persians, those of Cyrus's time, for their hardiness, and both believed that the Persian civilization deteriorated as a result of too much luxurious living. If that is the case, the Afghanis of today are in little danger, for their lives are as filled with hardship as ever, and it does not seem to impair them in the least.

He built some forts along the banks of both rivers, intending to keep out the Scythian tribes.

We know neither the month nor the year that Cyrus returned to Parsagadae, but we suspect he did not remain there long. Having traveled to where the sun sets over the Mediterranean, and to where it rises in the Afghan mountains, he was now ready to take aim at the center of the world, the glorious city of Babylon.

CHAPTER

7

The Center
of the World

WHEN CYRUS SET HIS SIGHTS ON BABYLON IT WAS ALREADY THE MOST venerable of Middle Eastern cities—perhaps of all cities in the world. Founded during the first Babylonian Empire, from which we have received Hammurabi's famous law code, Babylon flourished even more during its second incarnation. From about 650 to 540 B.C. it had no peer. Herodotus tells us the layout of the city.

> The city stands on a broad plain, and is an exact square, a hundred and twenty furlongs in length each way, so that the entire circuit is four hundred and eight furlongs. While such is its size, in magnificence there is no other city that approaches it. It is surrounded, in the first place, by a broad

68

and deep moat, full of water, behind which rises a wall fifty royal cubits in width, and two hundred in length. The royal cubit is longer by three fingers' breadth than the common cubit.

Herodotus also described Babylon's defenses:

The outer wall is the main defense of the city. There is, however, a second inner wall, of less thickness than the first, but very little inferior to it in strength. The center of each division of the town was occupied by a fortress. In the one stood the palace of the kings, surrounded by a wall of great strength and size: in the other was the sacred precinct of Jupiter Belus [Herodotus's name for the Babylonian God Marduk]. A sacred enclosure two furlongs each way, with gates of solid brass; which was also remaining in my time. In the middle of the precinct there was a tower of solid masonry, a furlong in length and breadth, upon which was raised a second tower, and on that a third, and so on up to eight. . . . On the topmost tower there is a spacious temple.

This certainly sounds like the Tower of Babel, but all records indicate it was of much later construction. We do not have to take Herodotus's word on every aspect of Babylon to be assured that it was a large, prosperous, and powerful city. But, as the Bible tells us, unless the Lord build the city, they labor in vain that build it.

This was the place Cyrus intended to capture.

THE HEBREWS IN BABYLON

When last we left them, in Chapter 2, the Hebrews (or Israelites) had been taken captive by King Nebuchadnezzar and brought to Babylon. There were three groups of captives, or exiles, taken in 597, 587, and 582 B.C. There were still many Hebrews back in the land of Judah, but their kingdom had disappeared, and, if we accept the words of the prophet Jeremiah, Jerusalem had become something of a ghost town.

Jeremiah, Isaiah, and Ezekiel (three of the most important of Hebrew prophets) all lived during the sixth century B.C., and their books in the Old Testament have much to say about Babylonian captivity. Let us begin with Jeremiah, who was not among the exiles; he remained behind in the ruined land of Judah.

> Thus saith the Lord of hosts: because you have not heard my words, behold, I will send and take all the kindreds of the north, saith the Lord, and Nebuchadnezzar the king of Babylon, my servant, and I will bring against them against this land, and against the inhabitants thereof. . . . And all the land shall be a desolation, and an astonishment, and all these nations shall serve the king of Babylon seventy years.
>
> Jeremiah 25:8–11

Nebuchadnezzar was Yahweh's servant?

According to Jeremiah and his followers, the kingdom of Judah and its people had sinned against God. They had retreated from what had previously been an uncompromising monotheism. Now they had to pay for their sins, and the Babylonian king was God's servant in the matter. This type of speaking was so common in Jeremiah's Old Testament book that even today we speak of a "jeremiad" as a forecast of doom.

The prophet Ezekiel, who was among the exiles in Babylon, also described horrendous, frightening visions of God that did not correspond to the Yahweh of the past. The God described in the Book of Ezekiel was like a warrior armed with lightning, but he was too frightening to behold, and it seemed that the people of Judah would continue to be punished for their sins. Ezekiel took some comfort, however, that Yahweh had chosen to show himself to his prophet in Babylonian exile; perhaps Yahweh would relent in the future.

Finally, and perhaps most importantly, there are the words in the Book of Isaiah that speak directly of Cyrus and his coming.

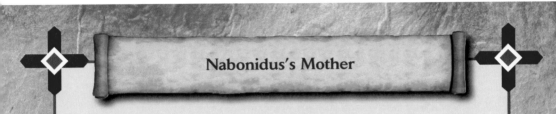

Nabonidus's Mother

She may be the oldest person from ancient times of whom we have knowledge. The Old Testament speaks of Abraham, Sarah, and others reaching impossible ages of 200 and over, but most scholars dismiss these out of hand.

In the twentieth century, the golden age of Middle Eastern archaeology, excavators found a stela describing the piety of Adad-guppi, a lady of the Babylonian court. Born either in 649 or 648 B.C., she was well into middle age when Nebuchadnezzar became king of Babylon, yet she outlived even him, long enough to see her son Nabonidus become king in 556 B.C.

The stela describes her as devoted to the moon god Sin, though it is not by any means certain she was a priestess of that order, as has often been believed. She may have been simply an important lady at the Babylonian court, devoted both to the moon god and to her son's career. She describes introducing her son to King Nebuchadnezzar sometime in the decade of the 590s B.C.

Nabondius seems to have inherited his mother's longevity; he may have been in his sixties when he took the throne and in his late seventies when he was overcome by Cyrus. By then his mother was dead and gone, but her legend lived on and on (she may even be the model for the Babylonian leader, whom Herodotus names Nicocritus).

SECOND ISAIAH

Biblical scholars now believe there were at least two writers of the Book of Isaiah, and they speak of "Second Isaiah," the author who wrote so much of Cyrus's coming.

> Thus saith the Lord to my anointed Cyrus, whose right hand I have taken hold of, to subdue nations before his face, and to turn the backs of kings, and to open the doors before him, and the gates shall not be shut. I will go before thee, and will humble the great ones of the earth: I will break in pieces the gates of brass, and will burst the bars of iron. And I will give thee hidden treasures, and the concealed riches of secret places, that thou may knowest that I am the Lord who call thee by thy name, the God of Israel.
>
> Isaiah: 45:1–3

Why was Yahweh, God of the Hebrews, calling and anointing Cyrus who, if anything, was probably a practicing Zoroastrian?

This is one of the perplexing riddles of Biblical scholarship. There are those who believe that the writer of Second Isaiah was practicing wish fulfillment and others think he served a useful purpose by paving the way for Cyrus's appearance. In either case, Cyrus holds a nearly unique position in the Old Testament; he is the only Gentile (non-Jew) called by Yahweh in this direct fashion.

The Lord of Hosts had spoken. What would Cyrus do?

THE ATTACK ON BABYLON

Cyrus moved against Babylon in the summer of 538 B.C. He had, by this time, a vast army, but it was not well coordinated in that there were Persians, Medes, Lydians, Bactrians, and others in his host. Very likely Cyrus had to employ a number of interpreters just to keep this army together.

This painting by Rembrandt depicts the feast during which a holy hand appears and writes the words only Belshazzar can understand: "God has numbered the days of your kingdom and brought it to an end; you have been weighed in the balances and found wanting; your kingdom is given to the Medes and Persians." Belshazzar was killed later that night.

Against him was arrayed the much more "professional" army of Babylon, one which had defeated Assyrians, Medes, and Hebrews in the past. Leadership of the army was given to King

Nabonidus's son Belshazzar (who is described at some length in the Old Testament Book of Daniel).

Nabonidus was back in Babylon, after spending a decade in the Arabian Desert, but he still seemed like an absentee monarch in that his son did most of the military and administrative work. Belshazzar had a very large army; he also held a string of fortifications that guarded Babylon on its northern side. One could certainly ask why Cyrus would not come from the south or southwest, but this does not even appear to have been an option. Perhaps the lack of food supplies doomed any attack from that direction.

By August Cyrus was in the northern reaches of Babylon, attacking the fortifications. There was every reason to expect Belshazzar to prevail, but Cyrus broke through at Opsis, on the west side of the Tigris River, and Belshazzar had to fall back. Cyrus was usually magnanimous in victory—one thinks of his victories over King Astyages and King Croesus—but here he showed a vengeful side. Opsis was destroyed and its large population was made homeless.

Belshazzar and Nabonidus were dismayed to lose their northern fortifications, but Babylon itself still seemed impervious to assault. Everything had been done, over the decades, to reinforce its walls and towers. Cyrus had fought many a battle in his time, but he had never come up against so mighty a place as Babylon (there was none like it in the ancient world).

As we saw in Chapter 4, Cyrus could be inventive, as when he used camels against King Croesus. He could also move with incredible speed, as when he snuck up behind the Lydians on the Cappadocian Plain. But a formal siege was another matter, and it could have dragged on for months, if not years, had Cyrus not made an ally of Gobyras.

A Babylonian merchant of some renown, Gobyras had been disappointed by the rule of King Nabonidus. Not only did the king neglect the annual New Year's festival but the merchants of Babylon had seen their wealth decrease during his reign.

Gobyras was probably neither the first, nor the last, Babylonian merchant to wish for the success of Cyrus, but he was almost certainly the first to revolt against Nabonidus and lend direct help to the Persian invader. Gobyras brought some Babylonians with him, but just as important, he brought information about Babylon's defenses.

THE RIVER EUPHRATES

Babylon had been built slowly over the centuries, and it now existed on both the east and west sides of the Euphrates River. Cyrus probably formed his plan before he spoke to a mass of his men, but it comes across, in the words of Xenephon, as if he came to the idea on the spot. "Friends and allies," Cyrus said, "we have viewed the city on every side. But I am sure I cannot see how any one could take by storm walls so massive and so high; but the more men there are in the city, the sooner they can, I think, be brought by famine to capitulate."

Ordinarily this would have been true. But Babylon was exceptionally well provisioned and well watered: The garrison would hold out longer than Cyrus and his men. Xenophon writes:

> But, said Chrysantas, 'does not this river flow through the midst of the city? And it is more than two statia in width.'
>
> Aye by Zeus, said Gobyras, 'and its depth is such that two men, one standing on the other's shoulders, would not reach the surface of the water, so that the city is better defended by the river than by its walls.'

Cyrus then declared his intention. They would create new trenches, of immense depth, and divert the Euphrates River. Xenephon describes the process in some detail. Cyrus's engineers and workmen used date palms and cypress trees to hold new earthen trenches in place and created "mud sills" so Cyrus could divert the water when he desired. All this must

Ander Theyl
Historischer Chronicken/
Inhaltend/
Die Geschichten der Andern oder Per-
sianischen Monarchy.

Von Ankunfft/ Geburt vnd Erziehung deß Königs
Cyri, wie er seinen Vatter Astyagem gefangen/ deß Medischen Kö-
nigreichs entsetzt/Ihme Joniam, vnd das gantz kleiner Asiam mit Hee-

ANNO
MVNDI.
Persiani-
scher Mo-

Because Nebuchadnezzer had been inventive in creating defenses that would protect his prized city, Cyrus had to be equally inventive to conquer it. He diverted the waters of the Euphrates River, one that ran through the center of Babylon, and attacked the city during a busy festival.

have taken weeks, if not months, and one wonders why the Babylonian defenders did not take more notice. Xenephon and Herodotus both assure us that the Babylonians thought their city impregnable, and that Cyrus was wasting his time. But sometime in early autumn, perhaps about the first of October 538 B.C., Cyrus struck. Even as his main army seemed to threaten the major walls of Babylon, a large detachment of Persians marched through a low riverbed, low because the water had been diverted into Cyrus's new canals. According to Herodotus, the Babylonians were in the midst of a major festival when they learned the enemy was upon them, both inside and outside the city walls.

The battle was fierce but its outcome was never in doubt. Once more, Cyrus had pulled the wool over his enemy's eyes, and this time the prize was the greatest city of the ancient world.

CHAPTER

8

King of Kings

CYRUS DID NOT ENTER BABYLON IMMEDIATELY. HE HAD GREAT RESPECT for its traditions and he wished to win the population over before showing himself.

Gobyras, the Babylonian merchant who had defected to the Persians, entered Babylon around October 10, 538 B.C. and became its governor. Gobyras made it plain that Cyrus would respect the gods, goddesses, and traditions of the ancient city.

The actual entrance took place on October 29, 538 B.C. Given what we know of Babylon at that time, and of the size of Cyrus's army, this must have been one of the most splendid sights and grand occasions seen in ancient times—perhaps the largest such celebration to that date.

Three weeks of Gobyras's government assured the Babylonians that Cyrus could be trusted. There were also thousands, if not tens of thousands, of other, captive peoples who looked to Cyrus as a possible deliverer. He did not disappoint. Entering the city, Cyrus went to the main temple to clasp the hands of the Babylonian god Marduk. Every indication is that Cyrus was a masterful user of religion and religious ritual.

Soon after he entered Babylon, Cyrus had priests or scribes create the Cyrus Cylinder (it was rediscovered by archaeologists in 1881). The cylinder is one of the few documents where Cyrus's actual words speak to us from across the centuries:

> I am Cyrus, King of the globe, great king, mighty king, King of Babylon, king of the land of Sumer and Akad, King of. . . . king of the four quarters of Earth, son of Cambyses, great king, king of Anshan, grandson of Cyrus, great king, king of Anshan, descendant of Teisper, great king, king of Anshan, progeny of an unending royal line, whose rule, The Gods, Bel and Nabu, cherish, whose kingship they desire for their hearts and pleasures.

Most royal texts of the time began in this fashion, with a rather boastful recital of the king's talents, glories, and inheritance. But Cyrus's stands out, even in their company, by his use of the expression "king of the four quarters of Earth." To our knowledge, no one had previously made this claim.

> When I [was] well disposed, [I] entered Babylon, I had established the seat of government in the royal palace of the ruler, amidst jubilation and rejoicing. Marduk the great god, induced the magnanimous inhabitants of Babylon to love me, and I sought daily to worship him when my numerous soldiers in great numbers peacefully entered Babylon and moved about undisturbed in the midst of Babylon. I did not

allow anyone to terrorize the people of the lands of Sumer and Akad and . . . I kept in view the needs of the people and all their sanctuaries to promote their well being.

Much of this sounds like royal propaganda. Did the Babylonians really love Cyrus? Or did they fear him? But he goes on to establish his claim as one of the first secular rulers who practiced tolerance toward other religions.

I strove for peace in Babylon and in all his [Marduk's] other sacred cities. As to the inhabitants of Babylon who against the will of the gods were enslaved, I abolished the corvée which was put against their social standing. I freed all slaves. I brought relief to their dilapidated housing, putting thus an end to their misfortunes and slavery. Marduk, the great lord, was well pleased with my deeds, rejoiced and to me, Cyrus the king who worshipped him, and to Cambyses my son, the offspring of my loins and to all my troops he graciously gave his blessing, and in good spirit, before him we stood peacefully and praised him joyously.

There is corroboration of this part of the story. We are confident, both from the Hebrew Old Testament and other sources, that Cyrus did set free the captive peoples. They were free to go.

RETURN FROM EXILE

The Hebrews living in Babylon were composed of three groups who had been taken from the kingdom of Judah in 597, 587, and 582 B.C. It is possible that a few of the original group of 597 B.C. were still alive, but most of those freed in 538 B.C. were either from the second or third exile group, and many were children of the original captives. Even so, it was astonishing to the children of Israel that they were set free.

The Cyrus Cylinder *(above)* is one of the most famous of ancient texts written in cuneiform. The cylinder tells the story of Babylon after the Persian defeat, and how Cyrus was willing to respect the citizens of the city, their gods, and also the gods of their slaves. This text indicates that Cyrus had rebuilt the Babylonian temples neglected by Belshazzar and Nabonidus, while also releasing the slaves from eternal servitude.

The Book of Isaiah claims that nearly 50,000 Hebrews picked up and moved back to what had been the kingdom of Judah, but most scholars believe the number was much smaller, and the first few years of restoration were not auspicious ones. Though Cyrus commanded that the Hebrews receive all the religious symbols that had been taken by Nebuchadnezzar, the Hebrews did not rebuild the famed temple for another 20 years: It happened during the reign of Darius I, son-in-law to Cyrus.

Cyrus himself drops away from the historical record for the next few years. This does not imply that he lost any of his power or majesty; indeed, he was greater, richer, and more powerful than ever. But it does suggest that he had premonitions of death, and that he wanted to set the new Persian Empire on so sound a footing that it would survive him. Toward that end he made his eldest son Cambyses (later known as King Cambyses II) governor and king of Babylon, while Cyrus went home to Persia. We do not know how many years had passed since he had relaxed, but we imagine that his homecoming was truly a joyous one. The son of a small-time king, he had become the King of Kings.

PREPARING FOR DEATH

To twenty-first-century readers it sounds ghoulish to think or prepare for death when one is only in one's fifties, but in Cyrus's time that meant a life fully lived. He had probably lost a good many friends along the way, either to illness or injury, and he must have been aware he could not last forever. If he was a Zoroastrian, as some scholars believe, it would have been doubly important to establish his final resting place.

Whether Parsagadae had yet become his royal palace cannot be said for certain, but we are confident that it was the site of much building during the decade of the 530s B.C. Cyrus had an audience hall built, complete with a throne room that enjoyed a spectacular view of the royal gardens. He had Lydian masons build what would be his royal tomb (more on that in Chapter 9). But most of all, he established Parsagadae as the site and symbol of his reign—the place where he had overcome King Astyages and set his own path toward international greatness.

Sometime in 531 B.C., or early in 530 B.C., Cyrus learned that his eastern frontier was under attack. Scythian tribespeople were attacking the forts and villages he had built along the Oxus River.

This action surely did not require the presence of Cyrus himself. He would have done much better to have stayed at Parsagadae and sent his best generals to the Oxus River. But Cyrus had spent most of his life on horseback, and he had defied the odds time and again. Perhaps there was a wanderlust that propelled his adventurous spirit. Whatever the reason, he set forth in the spring of 530 B.C.

TOMYRIS AS NEMESIS

The Greek goddess Nemesis was lame. In Greek mythology, she limped after men throughout their lives, to bestow a sudden change of fortune near the end. This myth gave comfort to those who had a hard time in life, and some unease to those who enjoyed good fortune, for Nemesis' hallmark was that she appeared unexpectedly, and changed things in the blink of an eye.

Cyrus had enjoyed excellent fortune through life. Not only had he enjoyed good health, but he had a happy marriage and several children. Not only had he managed to hold on to the small principality he'd inherited, but he had gone on to become King of the World, very much as the Magian soothsayers had prophesied to his grandfather, many years earlier. Now he met his Nemesis.

Tomyris was the queen of the Massagetae, a tribe that lived on the open plains north of the Oxus River. Cyrus had been here before; he had come this way in about 542 B.C., but much had changed since then. Like other Scythian tribes, the Massagetae waxed and waned in strength; this seems to have been one of their high points, when they could summon a large army. Cyrus brought his own force, composed of Persians and Medes, right up to the Oxus River where, according to Herodotus, he received a challenge from Tomyris.

It made no sense, she said, for the two armies to fight along the riverbank. Let Cyrus and his men fall back three days' march into Persian territory or she would fall back three days' march in her direction. Then they could fight.

Herodotus tells us that Cyrus was moved by advice to go north of the Oxus and give battle on Scythian soil. There was nothing special about the Massagetae that should fill him with

Tomryis, the queen of the Scythians, spurned Cyrus's attempts to court her into submission and refused to hand over her territories and people to Persian rule. Overestimating his abilities and underestimating hers, Cyrus attacked the Scythians on an open plain, and was defeated by Tomryis. When the battle was over, Tomryis ordered her soldiers to present her with Cyrus's head, as depicted in this painting.

fear; what did the conqueror of Babylon, Ecbatana, and Sardis have to fear from nomad warriors? But that was just the point. Cyrus had become more of a civilized warrior by this point, playing according to the rules. The Scythians, on the other hand, were very much like what his Aryan ancestors had been 500 years earlier.

Crossing the Oxus, Cyrus had a bad dream during his first night on Scythian ground. He dreamt that Darius, the 20-year-old son of one of his chief generals, wore the eagle and feathers of a Persian king. On waking, Cyrus went straight to Darius's father and demanded that he head home to Persia to make sure his son was not fomenting rebellion. The father readily complied and Cyrus continued his campaign.

Taking advice a second time, Cyrus left a body of his men where he knew they would be attacked by the Scythians. His detachment was overcome and the men were killed, but the Scythian warriors, as Cyrus expected, found their supplies of wine. Drunk and stumbling about, the Scythians were butchered when Cyrus returned with his main force.

Not only had he won the battle, but Cyrus had captured Tomyris's son Spargapises. Tomyris quickly sent a message, demanding the return of her son and the return of the Persians to the south side of the Oxus River. Cyrus paid no attention to the demand and Spargapises committed suicide as soon as his hands were freed. The stage was set for a final battle.

Throughout most of his military career, Cyrus had judged shrewdly and well, but he had a blind side when it came to the Scythians. His father, Cambyses I, might have warned him against fighting such nomad warriors on the open plain, but Cyrus was past any fears, in part because he had won so many times. The two armies clashed, and Herodotus describes it as the single most ferocious and desperate of all the battles of that century. All day it took, and at the end the Massagetae were victorious. Queen Tomyris had her guards search for Cyrus's body and when they found it she severed his head and placed it in a vat full of blood, saying, "I live and have conquered thee in fight, and yet by thee am I ruined, for thou tookest my son with guile; but I have made good my threat, and give thee thy fill of blood."

Cyrus, King of Kings, had fallen to Tomyris, queen of the Steppe.

9

Those Who Followed

CYRUS IS BEYOND DOUBT THE GREATEST OF PERSIAN LEADERS, BUT MANY other important ones followed.

First there was his son, who became King Cambyses I upon Cyrus's death. The son of Cyrus and Kassande, Cambyses had been groomed for leadership from his earliest years, but he lacked the free and easy style of his father. Not long after becoming King of Kings, Cambyses led an invasion of Egypt. The land of the pharaohs and pyramids fell to him in two years of campaigning, but Cambyses himself seems to have taken ill (Herodotus claims he went mad while in Egypt). Death by natural causes, in the year 522 B.C., left leadership of the still-new Persian Empire up for grabs.

DARIUS

Even today there is speculation about the exact relationship between Darius (about whom Cyrus had dreamed while fighting the Scythians) and the royal line of Cyrus. Was Darius a distant cousin? Was he simply an upstart? The answer is not known, but we can say for certain that Darius entered the royal line by marrying one of Cyrus's daughters (Darius eventually had a total of six wives).

Coming to the throne in 521 B.C., just nine years after Cyrus's death, Darius felt a need to demonstrate his legitimacy. The result was one of the most overwhelming of all royal

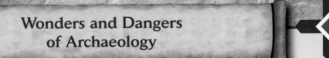

Wonders and Dangers of Archaeology

The nineteenth century was truly the golden age of Middle Eastern archaeology. Though many exciting finds were made in the twentieth century and though more still will be uncovered in the twenty-first century, it is difficult to imagine anything exceeding the delight with which the archaeologists of the Assyrian, Babylonian, and Persian empires went about their work.

The rock carvings at Behistun represent a very special case, of both excitement and danger. For centuries, millennia even, people had passed by on the Royal Road and looked up at the magnificent carvings, but, lacking telescopes, they could not make out the cuneiform writing underneath the massive carving of Darius and the rebels. Only in the mid-nineteenth century was the writing copied and translated by George Rawlinson. The danger which attended his standing at those heights and looking up to see the small letter carvings represents one of the fine examples of archaeological daring.

Impressions with the mark of Ahuramazda, the god of light and goodness, can be seen in Darius's rock relief. Because his connection to Cyrus was vague at best, Darius managed to establish his legitimacy to the crown by saying he was chosen by the Ahuramazda.

depictions: the rock carvings on the mountain at Behistun (modern-day Iran).

Even today, about 170 years after the first Westerner saw them up close, the rock carvings are simply spectacular. Darius is pictured on the extreme left, with his foot on the belly of a fallen foe. Nine other foes come before him wearing chains or handcuffs; this symbolizes his majesty and might. Interestingly, the one at the extreme right is a Scythian, revealed by his telltale hat.

Ahuramazda, the god of light and goodness, is pictured hovering just above Darius and the conquered foes. In the writing underneath the carvings (done in three different languages) Darius boasts of his victories, but is careful to give final attribution to Ahuramazda:

> Thus saith Darius the King: That which I have done I have done altogether by the grace of Ahuramazda. Thou who shalt hereafter read this inscription, let that which hath been done by me appear to thee true; hold it not for a lie [one remembers the ancient Aryan emphasis on truth in speech].

A bit later:

> Thus saith Darius the King: That which I have done I have done altogether by the grace of Ahuramazda. Ahuramazda and the other gods that be, brought aid unto me. For this reason did Ahuramazda, and the other gods that be, bring aid unto me, because I was not hostile, nor a liar, nor a wrongdoer, neither I nor my family, but according to Rectitude have I ruled.

That Cyrus the Great never mentioned Ahuramazda in his royal decrees has been taken as evidence that he was not a Zoroastrian, but it cannot be accepted as final proof. Cyrus showed himself supremely adaptable throughout life: his speaking of the Babylonian god Marduk, his sending the Hebrew captives home, and so forth. He may well have been a Zoroastrian who was content to keep his faith to himself.

Darius enjoyed many successes, but, like Cyrus, he took on one enemy too many. Herodotus tells, at great length, how Darius crossed into what is now southern Russia to fight the Scythians, only to be forced to retreat after they practiced a scorched-earth policy: wrecking the lands and crops as they retreated before him. Other than that, Darius was usually successful, and when he died in 486 B.C., the throne passed to his son, Xerxes I.

After Cyrus, Xerxes is probably the best known of all Persian leaders. This is because, in 480 B.C., he brought an immense army through Turkey, across the Hellespont, and into Thrace, on his way to conquer Greece. It is surprising to us that the King of Kings believed he needed to undertake such an expedition; it reminds us of Cyrus's feeling that he needed to fight the

Cyrus and Alexander: Were They Alike?

The answer is difficult, because we know so much more about Alexander than about Cyrus. But we can offer some tentative suggestions.

First, they had very different fathers. Cyrus's father, King Cambyses, appears to have been a careful diplomat, carefully treading water between the greater powers of his time, while Alexander's father, Philip II of Macedon, was a bold general and king.

Second, they were probably alike in athletic ability and physical prowess. Much is known of Alexander in this regard, and as for Cyrus, one simply did not become the leader of nomadic horsemen without being fit as a fiddle.

Third, their conquests were on similar pieces of ground. Cyrus conquered from east to west, then from west to east, then he took Babylon in the center. Alexander moved almost strictly from west to east, but, as with Cyrus, the taking of Babylon was a central moment in his career.

Finally, they were alike in that they both envisioned bright futures in which different groups and races of men would cooperate. The Cyrus Cylinder, described in Chapter 7, shows Cyrus's magnanimous spirit, and Alexander's mass marriage of 10,000 Macedonians to 10,000 Persians shows an effort in that direction. Both men were ahead of their times in that they envisioned the coming of world empires.

Although Alexander the Great had defeated Darius III in battle, he made an effort to ensure the leader had a proper burial in Persepolis, the capital of the Persian empire.

Massagetae in 530 B.C. Xerxes enjoyed a mixture of success and failure. He and his army fought their way through the Spartans at the Battle of Thermopylae, immortalized in song, poem, and movies over the centuries, and burned what they could of Athens, but the Persian fleet lost the Battle of Salamis, and Xerxes was forced to retreat. All the way back through Macedonia and Thrace he went, and, we suspect that he was grateful to reach the safety of Turkey at the end of this campaign. This campaign was the last launched by the Persians against Greece.

ALEXANDER THE GREAT

As mentioned in Chapter 1, Alexander the Great was, properly speaking, a Macedonian, not a Greek, just as Cyrus the Great was really a Persian, not an Iranian. Many interesting parallels can be drawn between the two men, not least that they were both conquerors of the known world.

Leaving Macedonia in 336 B.C., Alexander won a series of battles that took him all the way from Turkey to Egypt, then up to Iraq, where he trounced King Darius III in one of the great battles of the ancient world, fought at Guagamela. Darius III, a distant descendant of Darius I and Xerxes, fled the field and was pursued for over a year before he was assassinated by one of his own generals. Alexander the Great made sure that Darius III's body was taken to Persepolis for a proper funeral; Alexander then announced that he was the new King of Kings.

Alexander kept many, if not most, of the Persian traditions, and some of his Macedonian and Greek soldiers complained he had become too Asiatic for their taste. Leading his men toward the Lands of the Rising Sun, Alexander went through many of the same territories that Cyrus had: Both men passed through Bactria and Sogdiana. Like Cyrus, Alexander won nearly all his battles, and, like Cyrus, he wanted to create a world state, a unified empire. Shortly before his untimely death in Babylon at the age of 32, Alexander married 10,000 of his soldiers to 10,000 Persian women in a mass wedding.

The empire Alexander founded did not long survive him. Within 20 years it was separated into about five great principalities, led by some of his chief generals, who feuded against one another. The great synthesis, which Cyrus had begun, and which Alexander attempted to re-create, faded in the second and third centuries B.C.

10

The Shah at Parsagadae

IN OCTOBER 1971, IRAN COMMEMORATED THE 2,500TH ANNIVERSARY of Cyrus the Great; whether it was of his birth, his accession to the throne, or his death was not explained. Mohammed Reza, the Shah of Iran, also known by the title Shahanshah (which translates "King of Kings") wanted this to be the biggest birthday party Iran had ever seen, and for it to demonstrate to all the world that Iran had come of age as a modern power. Kings, queens, presidents, and prime ministers were all invited; after a few regrets were sent, representatives from 69 sovereign states, including 9 kings, 5 queens, 13 princes, and 8 princesses all arrived. U.S. President Richard Nixon was unable to attend, but he sent Vice President Spiro Agnew. Britain's Queen Elizabeth sent her regrets, but her husband Prince Philip and her daughter Princess Anne attended.

The festivities lasted several days, but the highlights were on October 16. Already at Parsagadae, the shah went to the Tomb of Cyrus to deliver this speech:

> Cyrus, great king, king of kings, Achaemenian king, king of the land of Iran, from me, King of kings of Iran and from my nation, I send greetings . . . you, the eternal hero of Iranian history, the founder of the oldest monarchy in the world, the great freedom giver of the world, the worthy son of mankind, we send greetings! . . . Cyrus, we have gathered here today at your eternal tomb to tell you: sleep in peace because we are awake and we will always be awake to look after your proud inheritance.

The shah brought thousands of top-level Iranian officials, but there were also costume designers and men who did historical reenactments of the time of Cyrus. The shah went through ceremonies that signified he was the descendant (not literal, but figurative) of Cyrus, and his reign was glorified in a way that recalled the pomp and circumstance of ancient times. Yet just eight years later, the shah was a fugitive, living in exile. What happened?

FROM PERSIA TO IRAN

Throughout most of its history, the land we now call Iran was called Persia, in deference to Cyrus and his Persian warriors who subdued not only the high plateau but also nearly all the neighboring lands. But nothing stays the same for long, and by the early twentieth century the place called Persia had clearly changed beyond recognition. The reasons were cultural, political, and religious.

By the early twentieth century, Persia was a thoroughly Muslim nation. What had been the homeland of Zoroaster

During the 2,500th anniversary of Cyrus the Great in 1971, the Iranian shah commemorated Iran's achievement from ancient power to modern nation. With extensive ceremonies and performances, the event was an international affair, with dignitaries and representatives from 69 different countries in attendance.

and his followers was taken over in the seventh century A.D. by Muslims, and there developed the long-standing separation between Sunni (meaning "Majority") and Shi'ite (meaning "Follower of Ali") Muslims that persists to this day. Persia became the heartland of Shi'ite Muslims, and its distant neighbor Turkey became the center of the Sunni religion. Whether one was Sunni or Shi'ite mattered a great deal, but there was, in any case, little room left for the followers of Zoroaster, who dwindled to a very small number indeed (some of them still live in Iran, but they number in the tens of thousands, not millions).

The people also began to call themselves Iranians rather than Persians. "Persian" implied one came from the province of Fars, where both Persepolis and Parsagadae are located, and this was too provincial an outlook for the nation as a whole. In 1935, Mohammed Reza Shah (father of the man who commemorated the 2,500th anniversary) announced that the nation's name would henceforth be "Iran," not "Persia."

Political considerations went hand in hand with economic ones, for in the 1930s, it was discovered that Iran had vast reserves of oil and natural gas. A land that had been poor for centuries suddenly was on the verge of becoming rich. For this, as well as other reasons, Mohammed Reza Shah tried to modernize, even to "Westernize" Iran. But he ran into trouble at the start of World War II. Known to be sympathetic to Nazi Germany, the shah was ousted when both the British and Russians suddenly invaded Iran. He flew off into exile in South Africa, but his son succeeded him.

The shah (this is the name by which Mohammed Reza usually went) made a slow start as a ruler. As a young man he seemed tentative, uncertain of himself. But, after the American Central Intelligence Agency (CIA) helped to unseat a popularly elected prime minister, the shah slowly made himself into one of the most notable autocrats of the twentieth century.

Using money earned from Iran's petrochemical industry, the shah modernized his military, becoming one of the most feared of all Middle Eastern leaders. He did not become embroiled in the Arab-Israeli wars, perhaps because he was such a good friend of the United States, which was itself such a good friend with Israel. The shah also flexed his muscles at home, creating a notorious secret police that hounded dissidents of all sorts. Aware that he sat on a powder keg of Islamic nationalism, the shah tried to assert one law, one leader, one faith on the

Iranian people. None of this was contrary to Iranian (or Persian) custom. Since the days of Cyrus, Darius, and Xerxes, the people of the high plateau had served all-powerful leaders: witness Darius's monumental rock carvings at Behistun. But the shah miscalculated the strength of Islamic fundamentalism.

KHOMEINI AND THE GREAT CHANGE

When the shah donned the clothes of Cyrus the Great and paraded his court around Cyrus's tomb at Parsagadae, it was one more indication that he was cut in the mold of the Aryan-Persian tradition, which had founded Iran 2,500 years earlier. Essentially, the shah and his supporters saw themselves as "Easterners," Aryans who had come from the east to settle on the high plateau. This worked against accommodation with Islamic fundamentalists who looked south and west (to Mecca and Medina, Saudi Arabia) for inspiration. Many Islamic fundamentalists said it was blasphemous for the shah to give such veneration to Cyrus the Great; he should, they said, have been giving reverence to the prophet Muhammad.

This split in the history and tradition of Iran (an east-west split) was nothing new: It has existed throughout virtually all of human history. Iran has always been a meeting place between East and West, between nomad and sedentary peoples, between Persians and Turks, and between Zoroastrians and Muslims. Given that the split was so severe, it is remarkable that the shah lasted as long as he did.

The Islamic Revolution began at the end of 1978, with massive demonstrations by students in the capital city of Tehran. The shah ordered out his military, but he did not wish the world to see a bloodbath; as well, there were soldiers who would not fire on the people. Toward the end of January 1979, the shah flew off into exile (he later died in Cairo, Egypt) and the Ayatollah Khomeini returned from Parisian exile to become the unofficial leader of Iran.

Iran's geographic location places it directly in between Eastern and Western civilizations. It has always served as a meeting point for the traditions, customs, and religions from both directions. In 1978, the differences among the Iranian people proved to be too great, and the Islamic Revolution began. The shah was exiled, and Iran, which has become an Islamic state, was ruled by the Ayatollah Khomeini *(above)*.

Seldom has so fierce a man been replaced by one even fiercer. The shah's power lay in guns, tanks, and the Westernization program begun by his father. At the height of his power, the shah seemed like a modern-day reinvention of Cyrus, Darius, or Xerxes. The Ayatollah Khomeini had no military power whatsoever, but his words and demeanor won the admiration of millions of Iranians. When the United States tried to push

The Hostage Crisis

Many Americans alive today had their impressions of Iran firmly stamped by the 444 days between November 1979 and January 1981, when 53 Americans were held as hostages in what had been the U.S. Embassy in Tehran. The impressions were real and important, but much has changed since that time.

Iranian students, most of them Muslim fundamentalists, seized the U.S. Embassy and took the hostages in November, holding them against their will. American President Jimmy Carter seemed helpless to free the hostages; when he did attempt a major rescue mission, the American helicopters failed to take off in the Iranian desert, leading to further humiliation. Throughout the 444 days of captivity, Ayatollah Khomeini became the most visible of all leaders, taunting the United States. The hostage crisis damaged Jimmy Carter's presidency; it also fostered the growth of cable television in America, where viewers suddenly saw the need for 24-hour news stations.

On the very day that Ronald Reagan became the new president, Iran freed the hostages. The former captives returned to rejoicing in the United States. No formal diplomatic relations were established between the United States and Iran, a condition that persists to the time of this writing. As a result, Americans and Iranians know little about each other, leading to potentially more conflicts in the future.

Khomeini, it met the fiercest opposition it had seen in decades. The United States, Khomeini said, was "The Great Satan," the embodiment of evil in modern times. Though he was a devout Muslim, and no friend to Zoroastrianism, Khomeini sometimes used words that were straight out of the Aryan/Persian tradition, describing Westernization as the great lie and Iran's Muslim heritage as pure truth.

Khomeini led Iran into a disastrous seven-year war with neighboring Iraq (1981–1988). Both sides lost millions of people in the fruitless conflict, but the losses did not seem to diminish Khomeini's popularity. When he died in June 1989, more than three million people attended his Tehran funeral, with thousands of hands reaching to touch the casket. Saint or devil, Khomeini had an extraordinary impact on his times.

CYRUS AND PERSIA

One could ask: Did Cyrus's career set all this in motion? Was he in some way historically responsible for the division between the nomads and the settlers, the Iranians and Iraqis, the Sunnis and Shi'ites?

The answer is no. Cyrus was a great man who, like other great leaders, seized the moment and rode it for all it was worth. Few have achieved such military success, and even fewer have known so well how to exploit their victories, with tact and persuasion as well as the threat of force. He was great indeed, but his life and career stand as a beautiful and haunting symbol of the historic splits between East and West that take place on the high plateau that we now call Iran.

CHRONOLOGY

◆ ◆ ◆

(All dates are B.C.)

612   Assyrian Empire falls to Babylonians and Medes

605   Nebuchadnezzar becomes king of Babylon

597   Nebuchadnezzar attacks Jerusalem (first group of Hebrew exiles)

590?   Possible date for birth of Cyrus

587   Nebuchadnezzar razes Jerusalem; second group of Hebrew exiles

585   Battle of the Eclipse (May 28) ends war between Media and Lydia

582   Third group of Hebrew exiles go to Babylon

562   Nebuchadnezzar dies; is succeeded by his son, Amel-Marduk

559   Cambyses I dies; Cyrus II (the Great) becomes Persian king

556   Croesus becomes king of Lydia

556   Nabonidus becomes king of Babylon

554   Cyrus revolts against Astyages of Media

551   War ends with Cyrus as king of Media as well as of Persia

548   Croesus of Lydia consults the Oracle at Delphi

547	War begins between Lydia and Persia
546	Sardis falls to Cyrus; Greek city-states surrender as well
545?	Cyrus campaigns in the east
540	Nabonidus returns
538	Cyrus conquers Babylon
538	Cyrus allows captives, including Hebrews, to leave
537?	Cyrus returns to Parsagadae
530	Cyrus campaigns against the Massagetae
530	Cambyses II becomes King of Kings upon death of his father
522	Cambyses dies
522	Revolts within the empire
521	Darius I becomes King of Kings

BIBLIOGRAPHY

◆ ◆ ◆

Ansari, Ali M. *Modern Iran Since 1921: The Pahlavis and After.* Upper Saddle River, N.J.: Pearson Education, 2003.

Armstrong, Karen. *The Great Transformation.* New York: Knopf, 2006.

Broad, William J. *The Oracle: The Lost Secrets and Hidden Message of Ancient Delphi.* New York: Penguin Press, 2006.

Burn, Andrew Robert. *Persia and the Greeks.* London: Edward Arnold, 1962.

Dougherty, Raymond Philip. *Nabonidus and Belshazzar.* New Haven: Yale University Press, 1929.

Fox, Robin Lane. *The Classical World: An Epic History from Homer to Hadrian.* New York: Basic Books, 2006.

Garthwaite, Gene R. *The Persians.* Malden, Mass.: Blackwell Publishing, 2005.

"Iran: The Show of Shows." *Time* magazine, October 25, 1971, p. 32.

Lamb, Harold. *Cyrus the Great.* Garden City, NY: Doubleday, 1960.

Nadon, Christopher. *Xenephon's Prince: Republic and Empire in the Cyropaedia.* Berkeley: University of California Press, 2001.

Olmstead, A.T. *History of the Persian Empire*. Chicago: University of Chicago Press, 1948.

Parker, Richard A., and Waldo H. Dubberstein. *Babylonian Chronology, 626 B.C.–A.D.75*. Providence: Brown University Press, 1956.

Rawlinson, George, trans., and Komroff, Manuel, ed. *History of Herodotus*. New York: Tudor Publishing, 1928.

Rolle, Renate. *The World of the Scythians*, translated by F.G. Walls. Berkeley: University of California Press,1989.

Romer, John and Elizabeth. *The Seven Wonders of the World: A History of the Modern Imagination*. New York: Barnes and Noble Books, 2005.

Saggs, H.W.F. *Babylonians: Peoples of the Past*. Norman, Okla.: University of Oklahoma Press, 1995.

Williams, A.V. *Persia, Past and Present*. New York: Macmillan, 1909.

Xenephon. *Cyropaedia (The Education of Cyrus)*. translated by Walter Miller. NewYork: Macmillan, 1914.

WEB SITES

The Cyrus Cylinder—full text.
www.cyrusgreat.com/content/view/16/2

The Cyrus Charter of Human Rights.
www.farsinet.com/cyrus/

The Behistun Inscription.
www.livius.org/be-bm/behistun

Professor A.V. Williams Jackson.
www.answers.com/topic/a-v-williams-Jackson

FURTHER READING

◆ ◆ ◆

Armstrong, Karen. *The Great Transformation*. New York: Knopf, 2006.

Broad, William J. *The Oracle: The Lost Secrets and Hidden Message of Ancient Delphi*. New York: Penguin Press, 2006.

Fox, Robin Lane. *The Classical World: An Epic History from Homer to Hadrian*. New York: Basic Books, 2006.

Lamb, Harold. *Cyrus the Great*. Garden City, New York: Doubleday, 1960.

Persians: Masters of Empire. Lost Civilizations series. Time Life Books. Alexandria, Va.: Time Life Books, 1996.

PHOTO CREDITS

◆ ◆ ◆

INDEX

◆ ◆ ◆

ABOUT THE AUTHORS

◆ ◆ ◆

SAMUEL WILLARD CROMPTON first heard of Cyrus as a boy and has long been fascinated with the story of this great leader. The author or editor of more than 40 books, he has written extensively for Chelsea House, including *Alexander the Great* and *Julius Caesar*. Crompton is a major contributor to the *American National Biography*, which is intended to be the standard American biographical source for years to come. He teaches history at Westfield State College and Holyoke Community College, both in his native Western Massachusetts.

ARTHUR M. SCHLESINGER, JR. is remembered as the leading American historian of our time. He won the Pulitzer Prize for his books *The Age of Jackson* (1945) and *A Thousand Days* (1965), which also won the National Book Award. Professor Schlesinger served as the Albert Schweitzer Professor of the Humanities at the City University of New York and was involved in several other Chelsea House projects, including the series *Modern World Leaders*, *Revolutionary War Leaders*, *Colonial Leaders*, and *Your Government*.